THE PRACTICE OF ENVIRONMENTAL DISPUTE RESOLUTION

Many actual events are described in this book. Those descriptions convey James Caplan's experiences, conclusions, and opinions about those events. Other participants in or observers of those events may have different experiences, conclusions, or opinions on how those events developed or about their importance. Mr. Caplan urges people with more to add or concerns about the events or opinions may contact him at www.environdispute.com. He is also preparing a book of case studies and asks all readers to consider submitting examples to him.

Concerning the graphics displayed in this book, unless otherwise noted, James Caplan prepared the graphics, obtained them under contract with Clipart.com, or copied them from federal or other public domain sources.

Library of Congress Cataloging-in-Publication Data is available from the Library of Congress

ISBN   978-0-9827537-1-2

Table of Contents

Acknowledgments

Cheryl Elizabeth Caplan, my beloved wife, strongly encourages my work. Her faith in me and in what I have been trying to accomplish simply makes me love her more.

My oldest daughter, Myrrh Caplan, graduated from Western Washington University, Huxley College with a degree in Environmental Policy. She always provides great EDR ideas whether as a student or as a LEED-certified environmental manager. My thanks to her for being a wonderful daughter and source of good ideas.

My youngest daughter, Dr. Eloi J. Hoopman, DO provides excellent advice about the medical model I use as the basis for the "EDR method that works". My thanks to her for being a wonderful daughter and interpreter of medical mysteries. Her husband, Neil Hoopman, an expert webmaster and software engineer, provides fabulous support in building our website www.edrusa.com and in preparing books for web publication. My sincere thanks to him for his expertise, patience, and clear direction.

Hans and Annemarie Bleiker, from the Institute for Participatory Management and Planning in Monterey, CA, www.ipmp-bleiker.com have been my teachers, mentors, colleagues, and friends for many years. Their pioneering work in helping agencies implement controversial projects, and my use of their methods, served as a "launch pad" for this book and its concepts. I couldn't be more grateful to them.

Established by the U.S. Congress, the U.S. Institute for Environmental Conflict Resolution www.ecr.gov of the Morris K. Udall Foundation is breaking new ground for federal agencies and their partners as they attempt to build ECR into environmental decision-making and management. The goals of the U.S. Institute for ECR are to:

> Resolve environmental conflicts and improve environmental decision-making through collaborative problem solving approaches (commonly referred to as environmental conflict resolution (ECR))
>
> Increase the capacity of agencies and other affected stakeholders and practitioners to manage and resolve conflicts
>
> Provide leadership within the federal government to improve environmental decision-making and policies through ECR".

Many of the quotes contained in this book came from Dr. Gabriel Robbins' web site: "Good Quotations by Famous People" at www.cs.virginia.edu/~robins/quotes.html.

Dr. Walt Cieko, Ph.D., BCIAC assisted me with understanding and interpreting psychological terms. For more about Walt's practice see www.waltciecko.com.

About the Author

Jim Caplan joined the USDA Forest Service in 1979 as a recent graduate of the University of Wyoming with a Bachelor's Degree in Political Science and a Master's Degree in Community and Regional Planning. Although Jim never entered a doctorate program, he earned enough graduate hours, sixty-four, to meet the basic academic course requirements for a PhD.

In 1980, as Jim helped coach managers during and after the Mio Fire in Michigan, Eastern Region Forest Service leaders asked Jim to write up his theories and guidelines for environmental dispute resolution, ideas Jim had developed in graduate school. Jim did so and he delivered Conflict Management and Crisis Control: A Manager's Guide (1980) to Eastern Region leadership just before leaving for a permanent assignment in the Forest Service Alaska Region.

In Alaska, Jim assisted regional leadership with public involvement and state relations, eventually becoming Regional Public Affairs Director. In 1987, Jim left Alaska for Wyoming, becoming Supervisory Land Use Planner in charge of completing the Bridger-Teton National Forest Land and Resource Management Plan. Then-Chief of the Forest Service, Max Peterson referred to the plan as "the most controversial in the lower-48." Jim successfully completed the plan and environmental impact statement in 1989 having garnered wide-spread public support and no law suits. Throughout this assignment, Jim used public participation methods taught by the Institute for Participatory Planning and Management and his own concepts embodied in Conflict Management and Crisis Control.

In 1990, he received an assignment with the Forest Service New Perspectives Team as Assistant Director for Communications and Planning in Washington, DC. When that successful assignment ended in 1992, Jim was appointed as national Public Affairs Director and served in that role until 1996 when Chief Jack Ward Thomas appointed him Deputy Regional Forester for Natural Resources in Alaska. Jim served in this role until 2002, including a one-year stint as acting Regional Forester.

Because of the Clinton-Bush administration change and political pressure in Alaska, Jim was reassigned to the Umpqua National Forest as Forest Supervisor in 2002 and served in that role until 2006. At that time, he returned to Washington DC as Special Assistant to the Deputy Chief for National Forest System, before retiring in 2007 to lead a Red Cross county-level organization for two years. While in DC, Jim rewrote Conflict Management and Crisis Control on his own time to incorporate more than 25 years of front-line Forest Service experience in environmental dispute resolution. Eventually two books evolved from that effort, The Theory and Principles of Environmental Dispute Resolution (2007, rev. 2010) and The Practice of Environmental Dispute Resolution (2007, rev. 2010).

Throughout his career, Jim won numerous awards for high-level performance. His list of publications is contained in Appendix C at the end of this book.

Chapter 1: Introduction to EDR Practice

Thoughts from Theory and Principles

Welcome to The Practice of Environmental Dispute Resolution. A companion book, The Theory and Principles of Environmental Dispute Resolution (Caplan, 2007, rev. 2010), presents an historical, social, cultural, ecological, and psychological explanation for why environmental disputes exist in America and why our current ways of dealing with them do not work. As I stated in Chapter 1 of that book,

> *Regardless of the scale we consider, I believe the world's single greatest environmental threat is not nuclear war, desertification, large-scale stand-replacing wildfires, or global warming and climate change, as formidable as those threats are.* **Rather, the single greatest ecological threat is the intractability of our environmental disputes and our collective lack of will and skill to resolve them**.

News headlines echo this message almost weekly, stressing the urgency of our situation and the glacial pace of our attempts at resolution.

To be successful at EDR, as presented in Chapters 1-2 and 9 of the Theory and Principles book, we must adopt the attainment of environmental justice and peace as our mission. Later Chapters 12 and 13 look at mid- and long-term policy changes and other actions that governments and businesses could undertake to embrace effective EDR and stop or reverse environmental losses and benefit businesses and people.

Long-term policy changes are needed but we must also act now. In Chapter 9 of Theory and Principles, I offer some ideas about EDR practitioner ethics and focus. In Chapter 11, I propose that we use a prescriptive model to support EDR practitioners and community leaders in gaining the benefits of EDR for their customers and communities. I base this model on the medical approaches of allopathic and holistic medicine.

In this "medical model" context, I structured this Practices book so that EDR practitioners and leaders might diagnose their EDR dispute and select appropriate means to address their EDR needs at any ecological scale. Accordingly, this book has the following three sections:

Chapters: 1-5   Dispute pathology, dispute pathways

Chapters: 6-8   EDR diagnosis, formulating direction, and applying techniques to resolve

Chapters: 9-16 Building, implementing, and ending the EDR program

Definitions for many EDR terms used in this book may be found on pages 183-184, Appendix A. Pages 185-190, Appendix B, offer worksheets to help prepare an EDR Program Plan. Throughout, this symbol ⬅ indicates an important point.

Understanding EDR "Pathology"

All environmental disputes are variations on the theme of differing values and desired outcomes. They manifest themselves as power struggles that may lead to negative consequences, even violence against people and property. When disputes are simply competition over ideas or outcomes, they are valuable and desirable, a part of American culture. When they escalate beyond a certain point, they can injure people and communities. At that "culmination point," unacceptable losses accrue and they become "**pathological**."

If disputes become "pathological," they seem to do so fairly early in dispute escalation — often at the transition from the issues stage to full-blown conflict. My reasoning is that, if issues are addressed adequately (called "issues-abatement") and as early as possible, disputants, caring onlookers, and other participants in the dispute do not perceive "unacceptable losses" taking place. As full-blown conflict emerges, people perceive that the losses of time, money, and resource conditions or uses are mounting and injurious to their values and lifestyles. Many times on-lookers more clearly understand the losses accruing than the disputants **who may be so intent on pursuing the fight that they initially miss the impacts**.

Please understand that **I do not believe that the people who are party to a dispute are "pathogens" or disease agents, or that they themselves are "pathological" in the sense of being mentally ill**. What I do believe is that **the way we handle disputes, our failure to embrace dispute-resolution methods and means, and our intentional commitment to win-lose approaches, can be considered unacceptably harmful — in other words, pathological.** In fact, I urge readers to understand this idea of the pathological nature of disputes but to never use the term in trying to achieve resolution. EDR is not about labeling or libeling people. Remember, the first step is always "**do no harm**" (See Chapters 10 and 11 of Theory and Principles)

My sense of the transition to pathological status is circumstantial and fairly subjective. For example, at the issues stage some disputes that involve significant levels of personal distress might create unacceptable losses for some participants.

Other disputes at the full-blown conflict stage may involve public-policy issues that all participants agree should be adjudicated or otherwise resolved. Therefore, they would likely agree that losses, although mounting up, are not yet injurious. In fact, many may feel that a crisis triggered by litigation might be beneficial. With this in mind, practitioners should be thoughtful about deciding that a dispute has become pathological until they test that notion with disputants and decide that an EDR opportunity is "ripe."

Addressing Pathology

The authors of *Contemporary Conflict Resolution*[1] speak to a strategic policy model. They propose that any strategy allow practitioners to "operate at all levels" with accurate intervention to create effective "denial response" — how to prevent issues and reduce vulnerabilities. They believe denial responses must fall within a policy framework that includes:

1. A "prevention strategy" to focus on issue management and education about effective advocacy
2. A "persuasion strategy" to seek effective means to redress grievances that do not result in gridlock
3. A "coordination strategy" to pull all the other components together to plan for and respond to contingencies

In broad terms, this thinking may apply to EDR efforts, particularly those at the full-blown conflict stage and at large spatial and time scales.

The authors of *Collaborative Approaches to Resolving Conflict*[2] propose a similar focus:

1. Preparation and closure — consult disputants prior to EDR design, bringing in history
2. Collaborative focus — drop power or rights approaches to favor interest-based methods
3. Encourage loopback options, providing information that gives disputants realistic benefit and cost understanding
4. Prepare and share a menu of options
5. EDR practitioners decide whether to serve as facilitator or mediator
6. Education and training to prevent recycling

In contrast, here is a restatement of my pragmatic EDR method from Chapter 11 in the companion Theory and Principles book. First, **do no harm**, then:

1. **Consult** the community and disputants to develop a dispute history and an understanding of current conditions
2. **Diagnose** the dispute stage and factors contributing to it and share that diagnosis
3. **Prescribe** processes and actions to address the dispute and gain informed consent [3] for proceeding from the disputants, if possible, before beginning work. As you

---

[1] *Contemporary Conflict Resolution: The prevention, management, and transformation of deadly conflicts, Second Edition.* Ramsbotham, Oliver, Woodhouse, Tom, and Miall, Hugh. Polity Press, Malden, MA. 2005. p.257
[2] *Collaborative Approaches to Resolving Conflict*. Isenhart, Myra and Spangle, Michael. Sage Publications, Thousand Oaks, CA. 2000. pp.163-166.
[3] See www.ipmp-bleiker.com for an excellent presentation of this concept for public processes

take action, use a "fishbowl" approach that ensures transparency and permeability for the dispute-resolution community
4. **Apply** preventive and holistic measures to address and eliminate dispute recycling
5. **Monitor and adjust** actions as warranted while communicating regularly with disputants and others
6. **Let go and move on or re-consult** with the community

Several places in this book will display the following figure to help the reader understand the subject being discussed and its relationship to the model.

| Consult Community | Diagnose Disputes | Build Prescription | Act | Prevent New Disputes | Monitor and Adjust | Let Go or Re-consult |

I suggest that this integrated "medical" model is sufficient as a process strategy for most cases. In some cases, however, particularly those concerning cross-cultural or international EDR efforts, the medical strategy may have to expand to incorporate culturally sensitive elements that change the timing, focus, and order of the work.

Diagnostic Matrix

This chapter introduces some organizing ideas about disputes. It describes them according to sixteen categories defined by four dispute stages and four dispute pathways. Although medical analogies are imperfect for EDR, the **stages** are similar in concept to progressive disease stages, such as those for cancer, with stage one the simplest and easiest to treat and stage four the most difficult. The four **pathways** define disputes categorically in ways similar to medical disease: infectious, neurological, traumatic, etc. To represent this diagnostic structure and help the reader keep various components in mind, I include this figure, often with color added for emphasis, in many parts of the book:

Pathway Stage	Distress	Scandal	Anarchy	Catastrophe
Issue	Structure	Structure	Structure	Structure
	Composition	Composition	Composition	Composition
	Function/Rela.	Function/Rela.	Function/Rela.	Function/Rela.
Full-blown Conflict	Structure	Structure	Structure	Structure
	Composition	Composition	Composition	Composition
	Function/Rela.	Function/Rela.	Function/Rela.	Function/Rela.
Crisis	Structure	Structure	Structure	Structure
	Composition	Composition	Composition	Composition
	Function/Rela.	Function/Rela.	Function/Rela.	Function/Rela.
Recovery	Structure	Structure	Structure	Structure
	Composition	Composition	Composition	Composition
	Function/Rela.	Function/Rela.	Function/Rela.	Function/Rela.

The chapter also describes EDR **contributing factors** that compare to medical history and disease symptoms. All descriptions should not be viewed as exhaustive, but rather, a starting place for further investigation and refinement.

Contributing Factors: Structure, Composition, and Functions or Relationships

Please see Chapters 4, 12, and 13 of Theory and Principles for a more extensive discussion and examples of ecological concepts applied to human systems. To promote understanding and undergird EDR practices, I add EDR definitions to match the ecological categories of "structure, composition, and function."

EDR structure should be considered the spatial, legal, and regulatory elements involved in an environmental dispute, including the legal aspects of resource ownership.

	Structure	Structure	Structure	Structure
	Composition	Composition	Composition	Composition
	Function/Rela.	Function/Rela.	Function/Rela.	Function/Rela.

EDR composition should include the physical and biological components present, adding to them cultural (moral, ethical, and traditional) values, the human-built environment, and the means people use for communications.

	Structure	Structure	Structure	Structure
	Composition	Composition	Composition	Composition
	Function/Rela.	Function/Rela.	Function/Rela.	Function/Rela.

EDR functions should include human-to-human and human-to-nature relationships, how one uses, works with, or changes another, and the content of communications as symbolic of and conducive to human relationships and desired outcomes. Functional and relationship elements include human uses of nature (sometimes called "ecological services"), the flow of solar and other energy, and the effects of human stewardship of ecosystems.

	Structure	Structure	Structure	Structure
	Composition	Composition	Composition	Composition
	Function/Rela.	Function/Rela.	Function/Rela.	Function/Rela.

Stage 1: Issues – Conflict Building Blocks

Description -- The initial stage of each dispute is the development of **an issue**. Usually constrained to a single topic or a few closely related subjects, an issue is characterized by differences of opinion or desired outcome.

Communication -- Often, the issue presents itself as a dispute over facts and a value-based interpretation of those facts. Many times, the dialog concerns the quality fundamentals of what is true and what is good, and the disputants are practicing externalization and transference of their internal issues.

Pathway Stage	Distress	Scandal	Anarchy	Catastrophe
Issue	Structure	Structure	Structure	Structure
	Composition	Composition	Composition	Composition
	Function/Rela.	Function/Rela.	Function/Rela.	Function/Rela.
Full-blown Conflict	Structure	Structure	Structure	Structure
	Composition	Composition	Composition	Composition
	Function/Rela.	Function/Rela.	Function/Rela.	Function/Rela.
Crisis	Structure	Structure	Structure	Structure
	Composition	Composition	Composition	Composition
	Function/Rela.	Function/Rela.	Function/Rela.	Function/Rela.
Recovery	Structure	Structure	Structure	Structure
	Composition	Composition	Composition	Composition
	Function/Rela.	Function/Rela.	Function/Rela.	Function/Rela.

Resistance -- Rarely do issues involve violence or threats, although the rhetoric sometimes contains diminishment tactics or disparaging remarks. These disputes often exhibit limited "triangulation" with third parties; triangulation refers to disputants making use of third parties to communicate, gain allies, or find satisfaction through biased intervention or power use.

Contributing factors -- Issues usually exhibit simple structural factors because they concern a limited number of topics. Composition is also simple because the facts, priorities, means of communication, or values in dispute are limited, as are the number of disputants. Functions and relationships are often strained, but communications content may still flow at fairly high levels of detail and clarity; disputants often see themselves as still part of the same community, honor their perhaps strained relationships within the community, and are willing to work together.

Practitioner notes -- In many cases, the dispute has not yet proceeded very far down one of the pathways, but some of the basic pathway indicators may be present and can help guide conflict managers.

Stage 2: Full-Blown Conflict, Wicked Messes

Description -- A full-blown conflict emerges when **an issue or cluster of issues remains unmanaged and dispute escalates**. A reasonably good analogy from nature is how a few lightening strikes can create multiple small fires that, if they go without initial suppression, can burn together and eventually create a fire storm, a huge fire incident that generates its own weather. So, similarly, a full-blown conflict is characterized by the complexity of its topics and multiplicity of its issues, its many advocates, disputants, and onlookers, and by widely divergent value sets.

Pathway Stage	Distress	Scandal	Anarchy	Catastrophe
Issue	Structure Composition Function/Rela.	Structure Composition Function/Rela.	Structure Composition Function/Rela.	Structure Composition Function/Rela.
Full-blown Conflict	Structure Composition Function/Rela.	Structure Composition Function/Rela.	Structure Composition Function/Rela.	Structure Composition Function/Rela.
Crisis	Structure Composition Function/Rela.	Structure Composition Function/Rela.	Structure Composition Function/Rela.	Structure Composition Function/Rela.
Recovery	Structure Composition Function/Rela.	Structure Composition Function/Rela.	Structure Composition Function/Rela.	Structure Composition Function/Rela.

Communication -- Often a conflict presents itself as a complex set of fact and opinion disputes, and although advocates and disputants attempt to simplify the values conflict, onlookers are often confused by the complexity.

Resistance -- Resistance becomes a prominent feature of long-term, full-blown conflicts, such as those between environmental advocates and public land managers since the 1970s. In these conflicts, environmental advocates moved from "essence" discussions about the esthetics of wild lands, through resistance, and eventually to officious bureaucratic and legalistic behavior. In their resistance, they found the old maxim to hold true: "to beat 'em, you have to join 'em." Disputants may be externalizing, transferring, and projecting their issues and emotions on others.

Frequently, full-blown conflicts will involve violence, or at least the threat of violence, and the inter-personal and inter-group rhetoric will display diminishment, ridicule, disparagement, and some blame attribution. Some onlookers have taken to calling these complex conflict situations "wicked problems" and characterize them as virtually unsolvable. This has not been my experience, at least not at the regional and sub-regional ecological scales of my experience. I suspect that the onlookers concerned about conflict "wickedness" are externalizing their personal struggle with the complexity of the situation. At the same time, I agree with them that once conflicts become complex and intensify, deconstructing and treating them is often difficult.

Contributing factors -- I also respect that some advocates and institutions exist to propagate and sustain conflict because they are paid to do so. Forest Service Chief Emeritus Jack Ward Thomas refers to such folks as "gladiators," an apt term. Gladiators fight because that is how they live. If they are wage slaves, these environmental gladiators fight to win financial security through client satisfaction. If free of wage constraints, the environmental disputants might fight for glory, public recognition, revenge, or loyalty to their constituents.

These gladiators are not necessarily a barrier to environmental dispute resolution because, at the end of the EDR day, they know that they will always have more battles to fight. For the third-party neutral intervener, they can be a potent source of energy, ideas, and values. Guided well, they will often assist with issue abatement, full-blown conflict resolution, crisis control, and managing recovery.

Full-blown conflict structure is complex and becomes more so over time because it concerns an increasing range of topics. Composition is also complex because the facts, priorities, or relationships in dispute are broad and increase over time, and because of the large number of disputants and onlookers. Functions and relationships often break down and communication occurs through third parties, including the media, opinion leaders, and elected or appointed decision makers.

As full-blown conflict reaches fairly high levels, disputants often see themselves as part of separate communities. Increasingly cloistered, they reinforce their values, beliefs, and behaviors and may begin to exhibit cultic characteristics: fear, isolation, blaming, and defensiveness.

Practitioner notes – Any full-blown conflict likely has proceeded down one of the pathways more definitively than a simple issue. Dispute managers should look for clear pathway indicators which may serve to assist their diagnosis and EDR program plan.

Stage 3: Crisis, Change Out of Control

When I led the fire-fighting efforts on the Umpqua National Forest in 2002, I had occasional discussions about "burn-outs" and "back fires" with my fire-fighting incident command teams. A back fire uses the winds created by a large fire to pull the firefighter-ignited fire towards a major fire to create a "black zone," denying the fuels in the area to the larger fire. Similarly, a burn-out consumes the fuels and creates a black zone but does not use the winds sucked into the larger fire; it simply burns a chosen site.

We used burnouts a lot on the record Umpqua fires, but because of weather and fire conditions and our proximity to private property, we avoided back fires altogether as being too large-scale and too likely to spread erratically.

We had not created black zones across the forest with "prescribed fire" earlier. Prescribed fire refers to fires set in advance of the most dangerous burning conditions. Fire is prescribed when burning conditions are right for reducing fuels and not likely to create catastrophic large-scale fire. We also could have conducted "fire use" while nature-caused fires were burning. Fire use refers to allowing natural fire to burn a particular area to accomplish resources objectives such as fuel reduction.

Prescribed and fire-use fires are carefully managed by trained fire-fighters and are often very successful. Occasionally, they burn out of "prescription" (or control) and create large-scale impacts, sometimes the loss of public and private property or even human lives.

Pathway / Stage	Distress	Scandal	Anarchy	Catastrophe
Issue	Structure	Structure	Structure	Structure
	Composition	Composition	Composition	Composition
	Function/Rela.	Function/Rela.	Function/Rela.	Function/Rela.
Full-blown Conflict	Structure	Structure	Structure	Structure
	Composition	Composition	Composition	Composition
	Function/Rela.	Function/Rela.	Function/Rela.	Function/Rela.
Crisis	Structure	Structure	Structure	Structure
	Composition	Composition	Composition	Composition
	Function/Rela.	Function/Rela.	Function/Rela.	Function/Rela.
Recovery	Structure	Structure	Structure	Structure
	Composition	Composition	Composition	Composition
	Function/Rela.	Function/Rela.	Function/Rela.	Function/Rela.

Description – Similar to wildfire under dry, windy conditions, crisis will occur if **a full-blown conflict intensifies sufficiently over a short enough period of time**. After a crisis, dispute fundamentals have changed often out of the control of disputants.

Communications -- Before crisis, the range of resolution choices may have been debated hotly over long periods of time and concern the old status quo. During and after crisis, resolution choices narrow down to relatively few and often define a new status quo. Through crisis, many key issues get clarified and resolved. Highly complex conflicts become significantly less complex. Casual onlookers may think little change has occurred, but participants often view the changes as highly significant and may communicate about what they, or society as a whole, have gained or lost.

Resistance – In a crisis, most communications are disrupted with little interaction among disputants. Some disputants may take the crisis as an opportunity for violent acts against property or people. Just prior to the crisis, some participants may attempt to trigger it through "rapid accumulations" of facts, opinions, and participants to cause decision makers to act or to cause functions or relationships to break down. They hope to achieve resolution in their favor.

Contributing factors -- The crisis stage is the point at which the structure, composition, and functions or relationships of the conflict may be irrevocably changed. When crisis comes about through a natural catastrophic incident such as a wild fire or a hurricane, the physical component of the structure is changed, and eventually the legal, regulatory, and social structure may also change significantly. When crisis comes about through a change in the legal, regulatory, or social structure, the changes often have less immediate impact because they are spread out over a longer period of time and mitigations may be built into the change.

A good example of this is the creation and implementation of President Clinton's Northwest Forest Plan, which greatly reduced timber harvests in the Pacific Northwest. The plan contained provisions for softening the economic blow and was later matched by the Secure Rural Schools and Community Self-Determination Act of 2000 later revised, which created an economic "safety net" that provided millions of dollars of payments to rural communities to offset the losses in economic activity.

Dispute composition also changes, sometimes radically, because the facts, priorities, or means of communication in the dispute are revised or realigned. Relationships are often strained during the crisis and can be lost or re-established as the crisis ends. Communications will generally be through third parties. As the crisis comes to an end, blame often begins to be a significant part of public and intra-interest communications.

Resistance -- In a crisis setting, inter-personal and inter-group violence (or threats of violence) are usually minimized, although some people or interests may take advantage of the opportunities that a crisis represents to harm their disputants or their disputants' possessions. In the later parts of crisis, personal or group blame attribution is likely to be the most obvious part of communications.

Practitioner notes -- EDR practitioners can practice the equivalent of prescribed fire and trigger a crisis early to prevent a later, larger loss. Other times, practitioners may choose the equivalent of fire use and allow a crisis to continue for a time until disputants and other participants are willing to work out their value-preference differences (called dispute "ripeness").

Stage 4: Recovery and New Beginnings

Description – Once a crisis ends, **a new order emerges or new conditions prevail**, things that mean a whole new set of emerging issues and human and natural resource needs and wants are in place.

Communications -- Communications will initially have a considerable component of blame, and it will be less about values than priorities and actions. Public expectations will include direct, effective action by government and private public-service groups, and public tolerance for broad-scale conflicts, such as those characterized by the full-blown conflict period, will be diminished. If public order has broken down, crimes against people and property may continue for a while.

Resistance -- Unless disputants have left the scene, the values of the participants will not necessarily have changed. Although a crisis is characterized by often-irreversible shifts in the structure, composition, and functions or relationships that existed before the crisis, issues and conflicts may soon reappear based on persistent and strongly held values. This shift of long-term values to a new context will mean that many issues disputes are predictable during recovery. Also predictable is the evolution of these disputes from issues to conflicts to further crisis if no intervention occurs.

Pathway / Stage	Distress	Scandal	Anarchy	Catastrophe
Issue	Structure	Structure	Structure	Structure
	Composition	Composition	Composition	Composition
	Function/Rela.	Function/Rela.	Function/Rela.	Function/Rela.
Full-blown Conflict	Structure	Structure	Structure	Structure
	Composition	Composition	Composition	Composition
	Function/Rela.	Function/Rela.	Function/Rela.	Function/Rela.
Crisis	Structure	Structure	Structure	Structure
	Composition	Composition	Composition	Composition
	Function/Rela.	Function/Rela.	Function/Rela.	Function/Rela.
Recovery	Structure	Structure	Structure	Structure
	Composition	Composition	Composition	Composition
	Function/Rela.	Function/Rela.	Function/Rela.	Function/Rela.

Contributing factors – As mentioned, after crisis, a new structure, composition, and function or relationship picture emerges. Structure will be determined by the new physical, legal, regulatory, and social order; and composition will emerge as people's values fit with the new structure and will include who holds power and controls the means of communication within the structure. Functions and relationships will be reordered, including communications content and communication networks.

Practitioner notes -- Many institutions exist to intervene and to deal with recovery. If public services break down, organizations like the Red Cross and FEMA step in. If public order breaks down, the National Guard can restore it. Counseling is available through many organizations for people who have to rethink and reorder their physical, psychological, financial, and spiritual lives. If the crisis was triggered by law or regulation, legal counsel and the courts are available to interpret meaning, and government institutions are present to put that meaning into practice.

It is unfortunately rare for dispute managers or third-party neutral interveners to build dispute-resolution capacity into emerging recovery-stage institutions. There exist some notable examples of such capacity building including "reconciliation boards" in South Africa after the end of apartheid. These boards were aimed at creating forgiveness as a key element of creating an integrated South African society.

First Pathway: Distress

Description -- This dispute-resolution pathway is often characterized by **simple, inter-personal issues**, although distress disputes can involve complex multi-party strife other characteristics of full-blown conflicts.

A distress issue might exist because a person is externalizing a personal internal-values conflict, or it may exist because the person is transferring or projecting their personal issues onto the situation or another person associated with the situation. The issue may concern personal object-, process-, or rights-related values.

Pathway Stage	Distress	Scandal	Anarchy	Catastrophe
Issue	Structure	Structure	Structure	Structure
	Composition	Composition	Composition	Composition
	Function/Rela.	Function/Rela.	Function/Rela.	Function/Rela.
Full-blown Conflict	Structure	Structure	Structure	Structure
	Composition	Composition	Composition	Composition
	Function/Rela.	Function/Rela.	Function/Rela.	Function/Rela.
Crisis	Structure	Structure	Structure	Structure
	Composition	Composition	Composition	Composition
	Function/Rela.	Function/Rela.	Function/Rela.	Function/Rela.
Recovery	Structure	Structure	Structure	Structure
	Composition	Composition	Composition	Composition
	Function/Rela.	Function/Rela.	Function/Rela.	Function/Rela.

For example, an issue could develop with an individual renting a Forest Service campsite and being unhappy when they find it littered with plastic bags and pop bottles. When they call the District Ranger and express their unhappiness with their experience, the person may be externalizing their own sense of inadequacy in dealing with the garbage they create in their life. They may transfer repulsion for trash that they learned through punishment from one of their parents many years ago.

They may be projecting anger about the situation on a campground host who comes to commiserate about the conditions, reporting to the ranger that the campground host was equally offended when in fact they were just concerned about cleanup. At any time, onlookers or family members may "side" with the initial disputant, adding to the complexity of the situation by their involvement and their interpretation of incidents.

When they talk to the ranger, they may generalize the issue and say that Forest Service campgrounds, parking lots, and pit toilets as a whole are "filthy" and offer further evidence that they may have accumulated over many years' visits. They may threaten to call the Forest Supervisor as a way to triangulate the issue.

As they communicate, they express their object-related value that visitors must have a clean site. They may communicate their process-related value that the ranger had not been following clean-up requirements and perhaps not enforcing rules and contracts meant to assure clean sites. They may express that, once they paid their campground fee, they have a reasonable right to a clean site.

Understanding an issue dispute on this pathway is relatively straightforward because the structure, composition, and functions or relationships are simple compared to full-blown conflicts. Structure is limited to a small geographic area, incident, or regulation. Composition is limited to a few articulated values, limited economic importance, the few people impacted, simple means of communication, and the few practices or behaviors being questioned. If a community category is involved, it is likely to be a "community of place." Look for focused, clear communications among a few parties. These disputes often exhibit limited "triangulation" with third parties.

Second Pathway: Scandal

Pathway Stage	Distress	Scandal	Anarchy	Catastrophe
Issue	Structure	Structure	Structure	Structure
	Composition	Composition	Composition	Composition
	Function/Rela.	Function/Rela.	Function/Rela.	Function/Rela.
Full-blown Conflict	Structure	Structure	Structure	Structure
	Composition	Composition	Composition	Composition
	Function/Rela.	Function/Rela.	Function/Rela.	Function/Rela.
Crisis	Structure	Structure	Structure	Structure
	Composition	Composition	Composition	Composition
	Function/Rela.	Function/Rela.	Function/Rela.	Function/Rela.
Recovery	Structure	Structure	Structure	Structure
	Composition	Composition	Composition	Composition
	Function/Rela.	Function/Rela.	Function/Rela.	Function/Rela.

According to H.G. Wells (1866-1946), *"Moral indignation is jealousy with a halo."* His somewhat whimsical statement reminds us that scandal mongering often represents self-righteous attitudes and behaviors, characterized by projection on to other people.

Description -- This dispute-resolution pathway can be **a simple name-calling issue or a full-blown conflict in which the principal dispute is characterized by a high-profile critic who castigates their disputant for being out of compliance with laws, regulations, or ethical and social norms.** The scandal monger calls upon the powers of society at large to punish the non-compliant person or group. The charge of scandal is made over one or two central issues but is often bolstered by many more issues offered as proof of bad intentions and conduct.

The central dispute is not so much about blame, although blaming is likely going on. Rather, the disputes is about the legitimacy of values, behaviors and actions in light of the scandal monger's different, sometimes stated as "higher," values.

Most charges of scandal are based on apparent differences between the behaviors of an individual or group and institutional structures, such as laws or regulations, or composition, such as poor treatment of the powerless by the powerful. That is, scandal can be about social or economic class behavior. Comparison and criticism dominate communications in such instances, and triangulation with third parties is quite common as critics marshal forces to demand their disputants change their behavior.

Transference, projection, and externalization can be seen in many of the contexts for scandal pathway conflicts. The complexity of these conditions can be very high, one disputant sounding much like another in describing non-compliant disputant behaviors. Resistance patterns often become clearer as disputants adopt tactics consistent with those they oppose. For example, if one party sends a legislative initiative forward, disputants will move their legislative sympathizers to block or change it. If one disputant takes out full-page newspaper ads, other disputants will do something the same or similar and attempt to escalate the conflict by talking to editorial boards to gain support for their position.

Understanding a full-blown conflict on this pathway is difficult because the structure, composition, and functions or relationships are complex compared to simpler scandal issues. Multiple issues imply many-faceted structural, compositional, and functional or relationship elements. Structure can cover many locations, laws, regulations, and social norms. Composition can cover the full range of values, from object-related values to the highest-level of Constitutional rights values.

Scandal often involves conflicts of significant economic importance, large scales of individual and community impacts, and the questioning of many practices or behaviors. Therefore, the dispute community can be quite large. EDR practitioners can expect broad, highly polarized communications among many parties and via the media. These disputes often exhibit extensive "triangulation" with third parties and often attract advocates interested in gaining real and appointed power beyond their tacit powers.

Scandal can be cried loudly, but this strategy may not be effective. Scandal mongers usually have to prove their assertions of non-compliance in some manner, although the means do not always have to be a formal process such as a hearing or court proceeding. Sometimes scandal is made effective through rumor, however, or in the "court of public opinion" as it is shaped by the media.

Third Pathway: Anarchy

Description -- Anarchy refers to **the rejection of established societal norms and behaviors by an individual or group with the intention of achieving a new order or status quo**. Anarchy is generally political and occasionally revolutionary in nature, but not often violent in America. Like scandal, anarchy is often pursued over a few key issues but can involve highly complex object-, process-, and rights-related values.

Anarchists can be focused on the past, or perceptions of the past, and these individuals and groups are often referred to as "reactionary" anarchists. They tend to espouse "traditional" values and use powerful symbols of social conformity, such as the Bible or the Constitution, as at least partial justification for their values, behaviors, and actions.

Pathway Stage	Distress	Scandal	Anarchy	Catastrophe
Issue	Structure	Structure	Structure	Structure
	Composition	Composition	Composition	Composition
	Function/Rela.	Function/Rela.	Function/Rela.	Function/Rela.
Full-blown Conflict	Structure	Structure	Structure	Structure
	Composition	Composition	Composition	Composition
	Function/Rela.	Function/Rela.	Function/Rela.	Function/Rela.
Crisis	Structure	Structure	Structure	Structure
	Composition	Composition	Composition	Composition
	Function/Rela.	Function/Rela.	Function/Rela.	Function/Rela.
Recovery	Structure	Structure	Structure	Structure
	Composition	Composition	Composition	Composition
	Function/Rela.	Function/Rela.	Function/Rela.	Function/Rela.

Anarchists can also be focused on the future, often expressing utopian visions, and these individuals and groups are often referred to as "revolutionary" anarchists, which is somewhat of a misnomer. They tend to espouse "progressive" values and use powerful symbols of ideas like social and economic justice, environmental purity, and aboriginal connections to the land.

Anarchists can come from communities of interest, place, fate, and tradition. They can exhibit isolationist or cultic behavior, probably because they perceive that society at large may not accept or support their views or actions. They may anticipate that sanctions will be applied by the larger society and live anonymously unless they decide to become change activists.

Most anarchy is declared based on purported oppression of an individual or group and by institutional structures such as laws or regulations. Anarchy can also address composition, such as permissiveness towards isolationist values and behaviors. An example of this compositional element is the level of support for bigamous practices by renegade Mormons. Anarchy can be about desires for the elimination of social or economic inequities, such as progressive anarchists' opposition to the World Trade Organization.

As with scandal mongering, comparison and criticism dominate anarchy communications. Triangulation with third parties is somewhat less common because potential supporters of anarchists realize that sanctions from the larger society may be imposed.

As with scandal, transference, projection, and externalization are common in many of the contexts for anarchy-pathway conflicts. The complexity of these conditions can be very high, again as is the case with scandal, one disputant sounding much like another in describing non-compliant disputant behaviors. Resistance patterns are often clearer as disputants adopt tactics consistent with those they oppose.

The media cover anarchy differently than scandal, however. In scandal mongering, media mostly closely examine and cover the non-compliant individual or group rather than the critics and accusers. In anarchy, the media cover the revolutionary individual or group rather than the institutions or individuals they want to change.

As compared to scandal, understanding anarchy is somewhat less complex because the structure, composition, and relationships are communicated in a less-complex form. Fewer, if still complex, issues imply structural, compositional, and functional/relationship elements that are easier to understand. Still, structure can cover many locations, laws, regulations, and social norms. Composition can cover the full range of values, from object-related values to the highest-level of Constitutional- and religious-rights values.

Consider the reactionary and progressive anarchists on both sides of the abortion issue. Progressive anarchists won the current Roe v. Wade compromise and defend it proactively. Reactionary anarchists are attempting to re-impose social norms existing before the Roe ruling. Violence has been committed by both sides, and confrontations are common. The core values of those involved in the issue include values about personal sovereignty for all American women and religious conformity by American society. Insofar as scandal is about a call for conformity, anarchy is about advocacy for non-conformity

Anarchy can involve conflicts of significant economic importance, large scales of individual and community impacts, and the questioning of many practices or behaviors. For reactionary anarchy, the range of these conflicts can be considerably smaller. Because anarchy challenges the existing power structure and relationships, dispute community membership can be quite large, although secretive. EDR practitioners can expect broad highly polarized communications among many parties and via media. These disputes often exhibit some "triangulation" with third parties. Sometimes anarchist movements attract advocates interested in gaining real and appointed power beyond their tacit powers, particularly if the anarchists are viewed as likely to prevail.

Anarchy is often not effective. The status-quo structure, composition, and functions or relationships often display a lot of resiliency. Anarchists occasionally appear to support scandal-mongers and a change agenda, and in this role serve as a "worst-case" alternative to the public and are represented by the media as such. However, conversely, tiny anarchist groups, such as Earth First! And the Earth Liberation Front/Animal Liberation Front, exert far greater leverage in environmental conflicts than their membership would imply if they act in concert with the more mainstream scandal-mongering advocacy of other groups.

Fourth Pathway: Catastrophe

Description -- Catastrophe refers to **a natural incident (such as a hurricane, fire, or flood) or to failures of human infrastructure (such as rail- and pipe-lines, dams, bridges, electrical grids), which can irrevocably change** the structure, composition, or functions and relationships that are part of the human environment and experience. The conflict comes from the effect of catastrophic incidents, often but not necessarily large-scale natural disturbances, on the human-built environment and people's values and expectations about that infrastructure.

Pathway / Stage	Distress	Scandal	Anarchy	Catastrophe
Issue	Structure	Structure	Structure	Structure
	Composition	Composition	Composition	Composition
	Function/Rela.	Function/Rela.	Function/Rela.	Function/Rela.
Full-blown Conflict	Structure	Structure	Structure	Structure
	Composition	Composition	Composition	Composition
	Function/Rela.	Function/Rela.	Function/Rela.	Function/Rela.
Crisis	Structure	Structure	Structure	Structure
	Composition	Composition	Composition	Composition
	Function/Rela.	Function/Rela.	Function/Rela.	Function/Rela.
Recovery	Structure	Structure	Structure	Structure
	Composition	Composition	Composition	Composition
	Function/Rela.	Function/Rela.	Function/Rela.	Function/Rela.

Catastrophes can involve highly complex object-, process-, and rights-related values — and these values-based conflicts change gradually in the aftermath of any crisis. Catastrophes often serve as triggers for scandal and anarchy conflicts, and for personal or small group distress issues. I have frequently seen catastrophes cascade into additional conflicts and issues, and so restoration efforts after a catastrophe must anticipate and address these potential cascaded conflicts.

People affected by catastrophe constitute a "community of fate," and they can also be dispute-community members. They often exhibit post-traumatic stress from the disturbance incident itself, and they may find their supportive communities of place, interest, and tradition lost or dispersed. A strong sense of victimization may spring up in some people and groups, accentuating values conflicts over ethnic, racial, social, and economic classes. Blame and the "tyranny of the victim" may dominate communications and relationships. Some groups have strong entitlement values that become prominent after a catastrophe.

Transference, projection, and externalization can be seen during and after natural catastrophes. The complexity of these conditions can be very high, one disputant sounding much like another in describing impacts and losses.

The media cover catastrophes differently than other disputes. In scandal mongering, media mostly closely examine and cover the non-compliant individual or group rather than the critics and accusers. In anarchy, the media cover the revolutionary individual or group rather than the institutions or individuals they want to change. With natural catastrophes, the media tend to cover the physical and biological dimensions of the situation and their impacts on property and lives — the stories are about death, injury, loss of property and relationships, and problems with preparation and prevention. In human-caused catastrophes, coverage will tend toward similar themes but will quickly focus on fault-finding and desires for punishment.

As compared to scandal and anarchy, understanding catastrophe can be highly varying because the structure, composition, and functions or relationships can involve very limited or highly complex natural and human systems.

Because natural catastrophe is imposed upon people and communities, people's emotions and responses tend to produce cooperative behaviors during crisis and recovery — this is sometimes called the "orphans of the storm" phenomenon. Natural catastrophe can involve disputes of significant economic importance, large scale individual and community impacts, and many past or present practices or behaviors being questioned during crisis and recovery. Because of the shared sense of threat and loss, communications are often less prone to propaganda or "spin," but they may be severely constrained by the loss of means or infrastructure

For situations of human-caused catastrophe, people may initially engage in strong cooperative behavior, but cooperation may quickly devolve into different "camps" engaged in blame and advocating compensation or official actions.

Use of the Next Four Chapters

Readers who have a sense of what kind of dispute they are dealing with, and want to dig in more deeply to their interest, can skip ahead at this point to any of the next four Chapters:

- ✓ Chapter 2: Travel Along the Distress Pathway
- ✓ Chapter 3: Travel Along the Scandal Pathway
- ✓ Chapter 4: Travel Along the Anarchy Pathway
- ✓ Chapter 5: Travel Along the Catastrophe Pathway

Readers who wish to explore all of the material in these chapters will find that each is organized like the others with description and examples. The reader can take them in order or compare them "side-by-side", section by section.

Chapter 2: Travel along the Distress Pathway

Dispute Pathology: each dispute displays a unique pathology in the form of structural, compositional, and functional or relationship elements; depending on these elements, disputes can be understood as <u>distress</u>, scandal, anarchy, or catastrophe pathways; disputes vary in intensity and complexity, from issues to full-blown conflict, to crisis and to recovery; for many disputes, unacceptable losses seem to appear as full-blown conflicts emerge.

Pathway / Stage	Distress	Scandal	Anarchy	Catastrophe
Issue	Structure	Structure	Structure	Structure
	Composition	Composition	Composition	Composition
	Function/Rela.	Function/Rela.	Function/Rela.	Function/Rela.
Full-blown Conflict	Structure	Structure	Structure	Structure
	Composition	Composition	Composition	Composition
	Function/Rela.	Function/Rela.	Function/Rela.	Function/Rela.
Crisis	Structure	Structure	Structure	Structure
	Composition	Composition	Composition	Composition
	Function/Rela.	Function/Rela.	Function/Rela.	Function/Rela.
Recovery	Structure	Structure	Structure	Structure
	Composition	Composition	Composition	Composition
	Function/Rela.	Function/Rela.	Function/Rela.	Function/Rela.

This chapter covers the journey down the distress pathway. For the distress pathway, and for each of the other pathways in later chapters, I present approaches for each stage of the environmental dispute: from issues abatement to full-blown conflict resolution, to crisis control and to recovery management. I will add to this material in Chapter 16, further discussing communications for each pathway and stage.

Distress concerns an individual's or small group's inherent values conflicts. For example, a man walks by an open shed and sees a car battery on a battery charger. He and his family have broken down by the side of the road because the battery in their old truck has worn out, and they are out of money. He previously asked the battery owner if he could use the battery on the charger to start the truck and get to town. He returned the battery after using it, and the owner began charging it, intending to leave the charger on for several hours.

The truck owner considers himself an honest man, and he strongly emphasizes honesty to his children, encouraging their honest dealings with others and punishing them for their childhood lies and thefts. And yet, his family is in a precarious situation, so he carefully shuts off the battery charger and removes the leads.

Then he steals the battery.

So, he has resolved a threat towards his family (family safety is an important value to him), but he has impaired his sense of personal integrity. He starts to hold a debate within himself about his values and his understanding about his actions concerning the battery. He engages in conjecture and analysis:

> Maybe the owner didn't need the battery any more and it was better used by a family in need (he applies his "utilitarian" value).

> Maybe the owner was wealthy and wouldn't care if the battery was gone ("avoidance of cost or negative effect" value).

> Maybe the owner deserved to lose the battery because it was carelessly available to be stolen (he practices externalization, transference, and victim-blame).

> Maybe the truck owner should have asked for the battery, but then, what would he have done if the battery owner said, "No" (lack of outcome control)?

> Maybe the owner was a mean guy and would have called the cops if the truck owner asked for the battery (avoidance of risk).

> Maybe his theft was observed and he was going to be arrested (avoidance of responsibility).

Months later, as he travels on his new job through the same area, he thinks about stopping to explain his actions and to pay for the battery, but feeling he would be embarrassed, he does not. A year later, his guilt significantly greater, he screws up his courage and does stop to pay for the battery by sticking 20 dollars in the front door of the battery-owner's home.

I was the battery owner in this example. My values are such that I was angered by the lack of communication at the time of the theft, and yet, I readily "re-assigned" the battery's ownership to the family in need. Of course, I'm only guessing about the internal dispute dialogue and emotions the thief went through. And my re-assignment is clearly a form of rationalization and submission. Still, I would have given the family the battery if asked.

This sort of values-conflict distress is common and has several predictable characteristics: tension between values or groups of values, communications break downs or avoidance, focus on blaming the victim or developing a rationale for victimizing, and a gradually mounting investment of personal thought and emotional energy into the incident and the relationship.

This last point is an important one: distress situations tend to "fester" and grow in energy over time as evidence is gathered, blame and victimization assigned, and rationales and ideas revisited and restated in an attempt to resolve the inherent power struggle within an individual or small group.

Distress – Issues Abatement

Pathway Stage	Distress	Scandal	Anarchy	Catastrophe
Issue	Structure Composition Function/Rela.	Structure Composition Function/Rela.	Structure Composition Function/Rela.	Structure Composition Function/Rela.
Full-blown Conflict	Structure Composition Function/Rela.	Structure Composition Function/Rela.	Structure Composition Function/Rela.	Structure Composition Function/Rela.
Crisis	Structure Composition Function/Rela.	Structure Composition Function/Rela.	Structure Composition Function/Rela.	Structure Composition Function/Rela.
Recovery	Structure Composition Function/Rela.	Structure Composition Function/Rela.	Structure Composition Function/Rela.	Structure Composition Function/Rela.

The issues stage is the point in the distress dispute that it is most capable of being resolved with the least effort — there are few issues and few participants. The values in play may be complex, but the stakes are not perceived as being very high so conflict energy is low. Positions are likely not fixed.

If the distress and inherent values conflict concerns an individual, then the individual can clarify their values and develop an appropriate resolution for themselves, such as the battery thief did in the semi-hypothetical example.

If the distress and inherent values conflict is owned by a small group of generally like-minded people, then the small group can put energy into clarifying what the issues actually are, having a values discussion around those issues, and asking clearly for issue-resolving structural, compositional, or relational changes. If the small group fails to manage the issue dispute, it will likely escalate to full-blown conflict, and then to crisis and recovery.

Here is another commonly occurring but hypothetical example: the Appletree National Forest leadership team is confronted with a challenge: a fish species, the orange-tailed catfish, has been designated as "threatened" by the National Marine Fisheries Service in accordance with their responsibilities under the Endangered Species Act. This has caused a shut down in the timber-production activities in the watersheds where the catfish survives.

Members of the leadership team know that they have to obey the law concerning the listing of the catfish, and they also know that they have to deliver the timber output required by Congress and expected by the local wood-products industry. The team also values teamwork highly and works to abate issues and reconcile any values-conflicts within the team.

The team members differ greatly in their values concerning the environment. Some members mainly support environmental protection and land set-asides such a wilderness, and some members mainly support development of timber, minerals, grazing, and other forest production to support local jobs and community economies. They have learned to rely on their diverse talents, values, attitudes, beliefs, and experiences to strengthen overall performance on the Appletree National Forest.

The team members feel the tension between the new protection for the catfish and their dedication to meeting their timber-production target. They decide that the issues they are exploring include:

> Where the timber might be obtained to meet the target

> How the catfish is to be protected and its numbers and health
>> monitored

> Whether they are going to be asked to restore catfish habitat

> How active vegetation management might fit into the picture, such as
>> the placement of logs in streams to create fish habitat and
>> restore watershed function

They spend about two hours in a values discussion about each of these issues. Although some members are very close in terms of the values they express, all of the issues have more than two opinions in play. The group had carefully articulated a vision for forest management a year before, and that vision is also discussed in the context of these issues.

The group members decide to gather some factual information about the first issue: the extent of the catfish habitat, and how it will restrict activities on nearby land, and the capacity of the national forest to support timber harvest in areas outside the catfish-habitat area. They leave the other three issues "tabled" because they know that many other people, not on the team or in the room, will influence or control the outcome of the issue resolution, if any.

A month later, the team takes up the "where the timber might be obtained to meet the target" issue again, and based on good staff work and mapping, they quickly resolve the location of supplemental timber resources questions. They then move on to planning and logistics questions about how to get actions underway to accomplish the target while meeting environmental-protection and long-term ecosystem-recovery responsibilities.

The Appletree team has engaged in issue abatement. If the issue was isolated to their area of responsibility, it would likely not develop into a full-blown conflict. However, the management team on an adjacent forest, the Sky Hook National Forest, confronts the same issues because they have similar habitats and the same listed catfish. This leadership team has the same range of values about natural resources and ecosystems. Unlike the high-functioning Appletree team, however, the Sky Hook team operates as a confederacy of factions that form one way for one issue and another way for others.

Under this approach, often one segment of the staff is pitted against another, and frequently, the field staff and District Rangers are in a coalition opposing the forest-level staff and line officers. The greatest contrasts between the Appletree and Sky Hook teams are:

> The Sky Hook folks do not have a strong shared value about
>> teamwork

> The Appletree folks have a shared vision that they use as the context for
>> delving into any issue

The Sky Hook team reviews the four issues. Coalitions build around each one. Faction fights begin during meetings and in the hallways and offices after meetings.

Eventually, the senior line officer, the Forest Supervisor, has to make autocratic decisions about how to proceed on all four issues. **Because the values in conflict are not addressed, the disputes continue in the background and implementation of the decisions is impaired by passive-aggressive behavior and turf protection**.

Distress – Full-Blown Conflict Resolution

Pathway Stage	Distress	Scandal	Anarchy	Catastrophe
Issue	Structure	Structure	Structure	Structure
	Composition	Composition	Composition	Composition
	Function/Rela.	Function/Rela.	Function/Rela.	Function/Rela.
Full-blown Conflict	Structure	Structure	Structure	Structure
	Composition	Composition	Composition	Composition
	Function/Rela.	Function/Rela.	Function/Rela.	Function/Rela.
Crisis	Structure	Structure	Structure	Structure
	Composition	Composition	Composition	Composition
	Function/Rela.	Function/Rela.	Function/Rela.	Function/Rela.
Recovery	Structure	Structure	Structure	Structure
	Composition	Composition	Composition	Composition
	Function/Rela.	Function/Rela.	Function/Rela.	Function/Rela.

The dispute intensifies and the Sky Hook team begins to revisit many of the issues. Disputes begin to intensify around two issues in particular:

> Whether they are going to be asked to restore catfish habitat

How active vegetation management might fit into the picture, such as
the placement of logs in streams to create fish habitat and
restore watershed function

The Sky Hook team gets locked into a series of faction fights regarding whether they should be responsible for restoring habitat (why shouldn't someone else do it, such as the state or the National Marine Fisheries Service), who should pay (well, timber harvest messed things up, so the timber program should pay), and should logs be cut in the restricted watersheds to be placed in streams or flown in from other sites on the forest?

The dispute escalates into a full-blown conflict, each faction fixing its position, blaming others, and looking for powerful allies to join the faction fight. The conflict spills over into the local community through contacts and rumors reaching communities of interest, place, and tradition, including regional and state-level groups. The Forest Service Northeast Regional Office (Region 7) gets pulled into the conflict by contacts from key interests and a couple of Congressional letters that spell out public dissatisfaction.

Region 7 leaders put pressure on the Sky Hook Forest Supervisor to "fix it," and he enforces more autocratic controls on employees and communications. The factions become more secretive and increase their advocacy, spreading the conflict into the Region 7 organization and assisting local- and state-level interest groups to enlist national-scale interest groups. Region 7 staffs add many issues to the discussion, issues about the overall management of threatened fish species, performance reviews, management controls and reporting, and media communications.

A Region 7 Deputy Regional Forester holds a series of teleconferences with Sky Hook employees and interest-group representatives attempting to abate the issues. Positions are now entrenched, so representatives of the various factions struggle to even find common terms for discussions. The participants will not acknowledge that their disputants have valid points and a right to hold their values, opinions, and positions.

After months of work, the Deputy Regional Forester gains a conflict-resolution agreement among most of the parties, but on the eve of signing the agreement, an entire bloc of interests walks out in protest, **having concluded that they can gain more by forcing the conflict into crisis through rule-making, legislation, or the courts. Collaboration has failed**.

In a short period of time in this hypothetical situation, the numbers of participants greatly increased, the issues multiplied as new participants entered the fray, communications grew horribly complex, positions became fixed, and autocratic actions and sanctions were used by disputants to increase factionalism. A full-blown conflict is the result and is increasingly focusing and consuming emotional and intellectual energy. Other work has to be abandoned to fight the looming "firestorm," a crisis.

Distress – Crisis Control

Pathway / Stage	Distress	Scandal	Anarchy	Catastrophe
Issue	Structure	Structure	Structure	Structure
	Composition	Composition	Composition	Composition
	Function/Rela.	Function/Rela.	Function/Rela.	Function/Rela.
Full-blown Conflict	Structure	Structure	Structure	Structure
	Composition	Composition	Composition	Composition
	Function/Rela.	Function/Rela.	Function/Rela.	Function/Rela.
Crisis	Structure	Structure	Structure	Structure
	Composition	Composition	Composition	Composition
	Function/Rela.	Function/Rela.	Function/Rela.	Function/Rela.
Recovery	Structure	Structure	Structure	Structure
	Composition	Composition	Composition	Composition
	Function/Rela.	Function/Rela.	Function/Rela.	Function/Rela.

As the conflict-resolution effort breaks down, the national-scale interest groups, both development- and environment-oriented ones, decide to make the Sky Hook issues the focus of their national advocacy and of their national campaigns. Congress gets deluged with lobbyists and the advocates for different positions. Protest marches are featured in the media, and serious policy experts discuss the issues on regional talk radio. One coalition provides notice of intent to sue to the Forest Service. Attorneys are mobilized and their advice sought.

Leaders in the Executive and Legislative Branches meet to consider what to do. As the conflict intensifies, several bills are introduced in Congress, but after two years and several attempts, no effective agreement on a course of action is found. One interest or another will not consent to a legislative fix because their values are not satisfied or because they are lost in the power struggle, and for them, winning is more valued than abating the issues or attaining other important values. Because it is so complex, the conflict cannot be resolved with legislation supported along party lines.

Back on the Sky Hook National Forest, the team is subject to greatly increased scrutiny as one lawsuit after another is filed over orange catfish protection and their timber program. The team falls deeper into factionalism, and some members are not speaking to one another. Blame deepens, and team leaders are frustrated by mean-spirited communications and low morale.

The President of the United States becomes interested in the Sky Hook situation. She visits the forest and calls a meeting of key leaders at the White House. The Sky Hook Forest Supervisor and the Northeast Regional Forester are not invited.

A month later, after consulting with a scientific committee and a Blue Ribbon panel of prominent citizens, the President issues her Executive Order and Plan that set the boundaries for timber harvest and habitat protection on seven national forests, including the Appletree and Sky Hook units.

➡ The full-blown conflict has **escalated to a crisis, irreversible change has occurred** through an autocratic decision, and a new set of requirements are now in place and form part of the structure and context for future issues.

Distress – Managing Recovery

Pathway Stage	Distress	Scandal	Anarchy	Catastrophe
Issue	Structure	Structure	Structure	Structure
	Composition	Composition	Composition	Composition
	Function/Rela.	Function/Rela.	Function/Rela.	Function/Rela.
Full-blown Conflict	Structure	Structure	Structure	Structure
	Composition	Composition	Composition	Composition
	Function/Rela.	Function/Rela.	Function/Rela.	Function/Rela.
Crisis	Structure	Structure	Structure	Structure
	Composition	Composition	Composition	Composition
	Function/Rela.	Function/Rela.	Function/Rela.	Function/Rela.
Recovery	Structure	Structure	Structure	Structure
	Composition	Composition	Composition	Composition
	Function/Rela.	Function/Rela.	Function/Rela.	Function/Rela.

By contrast, on the Appletree National Forest, recovery in the aftermath of crisis proceeds smoothly. The leadership team regrets the confusion and disruption of it service delivery, but the members now understand that the President's decision clarifies how all four issues they were struggling with can be resolved.

The Appletree team sets up a series of community meetings and intense working meetings with interest groups to discuss implementation. They begin to populate the new dispute structure with communications, processes, and methods designed to make sure key issues and interest-group values get addressed on a continuous basis; they gather volunteers and supporters for these efforts, which include monitoring field trips, scientific reviews by university and Forest Service scientists, and volunteer-led communications using newsletters and the media.

Meanwhile, the Sky Hook team continues to struggle with the factional fighting, the casting of blame, and issue implementation; but the team is encouraged that the law suits over its programs seem to be diminishing and work can move ahead with less internal and external resistance. The team begins recovery with the idea that "they are the professionals and know what's best."

They communicate with the public through press releases about program and project adjustments and through their National Environmental Policy Act "notice and comment" efforts. They populate the new dispute structure with routine processes and do not notice that the disputes that grew out of the original issue continue to go unaddressed both inside and outside the unit.

Chapter 3: Travel along the Scandal Pathway

Dispute Pathology: each dispute displays a unique pathology in the form of structural, compositional, and functional or relationship elements; depending on these elements, disputes can be understood as distress, scandal, anarchy, or catastrophe pathways; disputes vary in intensity and complexity from issues to full-blown conflict, to crisis and to recovery; for many disputes, unacceptable losses seem to appear as full-blown conflicts emerge.

Pathway Stage	Distress	Scandal	Anarchy	Catastrophe
Issue	Structure	Structure	Structure	Structure
	Composition	Composition	Composition	Composition
	Function/Rela.	Function/Rela.	Function/Rela.	Function/Rela.
Full-blown Conflict	Structure	Structure	Structure	Structure
	Composition	Composition	Composition	Composition
	Function/Rela.	Function/Rela.	Function/Rela.	Function/Rela.
Crisis	Structure	Structure	Structure	Structure
	Composition	Composition	Composition	Composition
	Function/Rela.	Function/Rela.	Function/Rela.	Function/Rela.
Recovery	Structure	Structure	Structure	Structure
	Composition	Composition	Composition	Composition
	Function/Rela.	Function/Rela.	Function/Rela.	Function/Rela.

This chapter covers the journey along the scandal pathway. Scandal refers to an attempt by one party to enforce laws, regulations, rules, ethics, morals, or societal norms upon another party. Disputants attempt to do this **in conjunction with communications that contain accusations or allegations, blaming and attempted shaming**.

The phrase that describes this action and communications is "crying scandal." The person taking the action is a "scandalmonger." The scandalmonger focuses on exposing the allegedly illegal, unethical, immoral, or socially disruptive behavior or actions of their disputants. Like all other disputes, the conflict is a values conflict and concerns power and control. Scandals are either "effective" or "ineffective," depending on whether they actually change behaviors or exert control over incidents.

Scandal mongering is probably as old as the human race. For example, scandal appears as one of the first stories in the Holy Bible in the book of Genesis. Adam and Eve violate the rules of Eden, feel shame, and hide from God. Judged guilty for their loss of innocence, God evicts them.[4] In a more modern context, scandal is the basis for the plot in *The Scarlet Letter,*[5] a mainstay of high school English literature studies, but the proof

---

[4] *The Amplified Bible,* Genesis: Chapters 1-3. Zondervan Bible Publishers. Grand Rapids, MI. 1982.
[5] *The Scarlet Letter.* Hawthorne, Nathaniel. 1850.

of scandal in our daily lives is much more readily available than fiction. You can read any major newspaper for the lurid and contemporary versions of this very human theme.

For the EDR practitioner, the presence of scandal mongering is a key indicator of the nature of the dispute, and more importantly, it is a key to understanding the methods and means one disputant has chosen to try to control the other. To be effective in managing a scandal-based and scandal-driven dispute, the EDR practitioner must first recognize it, diagnose it, and then prescribe effective remedies.

Unfortunately, as Sir Winston Churchill (1874-1965) said, "A lie gets halfway around the world before the truth has a chance to get its pants on." So, EDR practitioners and people who are the subject of scandal have some serious work to do to help truth "get its pants on" and "catch up" with any misinformation, exaggeration, or outright lie.

Crying scandal is **manifested as one of two types**. The first focuses on violations of laws, regulations, rules, or professional ethics — these speak to the illegitimacy of someone's behavior or actions in light of a written code or requirements and often refer to structural, and sometimes compositional, aspects of the dispute. The argument is often expressed in terms of "legal" versus "illegal" by the scandalmonger.

The second type of scandal focuses on perceived violations of personal ethics, morals, agreements, or group norms as expressed as principles, such as compliance with the tenets of religion. Scandalmongers of this type often refer to compositional or relationship aspects of the dispute, and this argument is often expressed in terms of "right" versus "wrong." Scandalmongers often try to portray the ethical or moral issues in "black or white," or "good versus evil," terms.

The two types can manifest together and add to confusion about EDR approaches (but more on that phenomenon later). Both types of scandal mongering focus on purported values violations but address different values, societal-legal or personal-moral. The people crying scandal about a violation of a written code have a point of reference, and they likely have precedents and institutions like the court system to use in pursing their action-correction interests. Many interest groups pursue lawsuits and surround their legal advocacy with communications that claim violations of laws and regulations, and they then attempt to focus social and political pressure through shaming. Sanctions for an effective scandal can include criminal and civil penalties and changes in public policy, funding, and leadership.

I refer to this type of scandal mongering as **"crying institutional scandal"** because the scandalmonger focuses on formal, often "legalese" messages as the means to exert power or control. Institutional scandal mongers, media, and caring onlookers are often concerned with "what did they know," "when did they know it," and "what did they do about it?"

People crying scandal about perceived violations of group norms, morals or ethics often base their allegations on more ambiguous concepts, such as unmet expectations for honesty, fidelity, fairness, piety, trust, or compassion. These violations concern values that perhaps evoke a stronger emotional response from onlookers than the subject of institutional scandal. The scandalmongers may have some recourse to the courts or other institutions, but they are more likely to pursue their goals through informal means, such as person-to-person networks within organizations or communities, the media, or extended family connections.

I refer to this type of scandal mongering **as "crying moral scandal"** because the scandalmonger focuses on informal, often hard-to-define standards, and imputes negative or unacceptable moral values or beliefs to disputants. As Alice Roosevelt Longworth (1884-1980) once said, referring to the salacious nature of this kind of scandal, *"If you haven't got anything nice to say about anybody, come sit next to me."* The moral scandalmonger attempts to control through social sanctions, such as ostracism, ridicule, loss of status, or diminishment. Gossip and rumors are often mechanisms employed by the moral scandalmonger. Questions that get asked cover subjects such as "what did they do," "who was harmed," "did they break the law," "did they violate ethics," "did they violate morals or standards of propriety," or "did they damage inter-personal functions or relationships?"

Effective moral scandal can also result in loss of employment or loss of relationships, as in a divorce or end of a friendship. Moral scandal mongering often focuses on public figures, such as candidates for political office, and can be a major factor in swaying public opinion and determining election results.

Issues Abatement along the Scandal Pathway

Pathway Stage	Distress	Scandal	Anarchy	Catastrophe
Issue	Structure	Structure	Structure	Structure
	Composition	Composition	Composition	Composition
	Function/Rela.	Function/Rela.	Function/Rela.	Function/Rela.
Full-blown Conflict	Structure	Structure	Structure	Structure
	Composition	Composition	Composition	Composition
	Function/Rela.	Function/Rela.	Function/Rela.	Function/Rela.
Crisis	Structure	Structure	Structure	Structure
	Composition	Composition	Composition	Composition
	Function/Rela.	Function/Rela.	Function/Rela.	Function/Rela.
Recovery	Structure	Structure	Structure	Structure
	Composition	Composition	Composition	Composition
	Function/Rela.	Function/Rela.	Function/Rela.	Function/Rela.

Scandal often presents as a "shotgun blast" of accusations — a confusing mixture of institutional and moral scandal mongering. But at the issues stage, usually one allegation is most clear and prominent. In EDR work, practitioners will find that sorting out which types are present and clarifying the specific allegations is quite important.

The scandalmonger's thoughts and positions are important, of course, but so are the thoughts and positions of the target individual or small group. Sometimes, the media or uninvolved but caring onlookers are also useful as well, particularly to help define the key issues raised and their relative importance.

As an example, the Forest Service observed its Centennial in 2005. Activities and celebrations occurred across the U.S. Vendors offered Centennial products to present and former employees and the public. I led a small ad hoc team established by the National Headquarters to assist firearms manufacturers with product-approval processes and rifle design, emphasizing historic themes. NyeKass Arms of Nixa, Missouri decided to produce a Centennial rifle and, later, a pistol.

As the time for the announcement of the rifle's availability came, I contacted Centennial coordinators at the National Headquarters and asked how they would like to make information about the rifle available to Forest Service employees, past and present. Headquarters told me to communicate the availability myself.

I sent an e-mail to leadership teams across the country that explicitly stated that the Forest Service did not endorse any product or manufacturer and that interested employees could access the NyeKass website for any further information. The e-mail had been in circulation a couple of days when I got a call from the "Mission Area Ethics Advisor" for the Forest Service, who questioned me about my role in the production of and communication about the Centennial rifle. One of the e-mail recipients had contacted the Advisor, asking if my communication was ethical. The Advisor quickly issued a memo sent nationwide condemning my action as unethical. In doing this, the Advisor cried institutional scandal using generalized condemnation (basically stating "this is unethical") without supporting citations or information. Because the Advisor sent the message nationwide, and I quickly received e-mails of both blame and support from employees across the country.

Because the Advisor represented structural authority, if the scandal was effective, I was subject to sanctions, including potentially being fined or fired. Because the Advisor also represented the more formal aspects of compositional and relationship factors (although with much less force than the structural aspects the Advisor represented), I was also subject to loss of reputation, loss of job opportunities, and ostracism or ridicule.

Before attempting to resolve my dispute with the Advisor, I had to ascertain what structural, compositional, and functional or relationship factors were present that might define the scandal and make it effective or ineffective.

From a structural standpoint, I reviewed the ethics requirements from the federal Office of Government Ethics and USDA and Forest Service ethics directives. I found no support for the Advisor's position. I sent a memo to the National Headquarters detailing my findings and asking for a response confirming my analysis and reversing the Advisor's opinion. I also asked that National Headquarters' staff communicate the response to Forest Service employees.

From a compositional standpoint, I discovered that there were ongoing disputes between field ethics advisors and the Mission Area Ethics Advisor over interpretation of ethics directives. Specifically, the field advisors could not find the basis for many of the Advisor's opinions in law or regulation. They felt that too many Advisor opinions were needlessly vague, restrictive, and unsupportable. From a relationship standpoint, I found that the majority of my colleagues thought the scandal was ineffective. They thought that the direction from the National Headquarters that I should release the information about the rifle meant that any ethics concerns might be more appropriately pursued among the staffs in Washington, DC and not with someone working for them at a field location like myself.

I expected my memo to confront and eliminate the structural issues. I also anticipated the correction from the National Headquarters to address the informal compositional and relationship issues.

Months went by. Finally, the National Headquarters staff issued a memo to field ethics advisors (not to me or to the people on the Advisor's original e-mail list) clearing me of wrongdoing but implying that I had created an "appearance of conflict of interest," another allegation and conclusion not consistent with ethics directives. However, the passage of time and contacts with field people indicated to me that the institutional and moral scandal mongering had both been ineffective, and that I needed to take no further action to resolve the dispute.

Resolving Full-Blown Conflict along the Scandal Pathway

Pathway Stage	Distress	Scandal	Anarchy	Catastrophe
Issue	Structure	Structure	Structure	Structure
	Composition	Composition	Composition	Composition
	Function/Rela.	Function/Rela.	Function/Rela.	Function/Rela.
Full-blown Conflict	Structure	Structure	Structure	Structure
	Composition	Composition	Composition	Composition
	Function/Rela.	Function/Rela.	Function/Rela.	Function/Rela.
Crisis	Structure	Structure	Structure	Structure
	Composition	Composition	Composition	Composition
	Function/Rela.	Function/Rela.	Function/Rela.	Function/Rela.
Recovery	Structure	Structure	Structure	Structure
	Composition	Composition	Composition	Composition
	Function/Rela.	Function/Rela.	Function/Rela.	Function/Rela.

If I had not been able to render ineffective the scandals cried against me, a full-blown conflict could have emerged in which the Forest Service would have followed employee-relations investigative procedure. Specialists would have conducted a formal investigation. Line officers would perhaps have issued charges against me and proposed removal or some lesser penalty.

I could have countered with a separate investigation and allegations, requests for Congressional oversight and intervention, and press releases or other communications to rally supporters. The issues and players would have become a complex mix as appointed officials, attorneys, and elected officials began to weigh in. Communications would get difficult both because of the formality of the processes and because so many people with differing values, interests, and intentions would be involved. Time scale would have become prolonged by process timelines and procedural advocacy from my attorneys.

Happily, that did not have to happen because the conflict was managed as what it was: a few issues that were disputed among few disputants with limited communications.

The firefighting efforts that I led on the Umpqua National Forest in 2002 serve as EDR example of full-blown conflict resolution. Those record fires burned about 9% of the forest, varying from low- to high-intensity, covering all the acreage that had previously burned in small annual amounts between 1939 and 2001. While the fires were still burning, employees were working in the blackened areas to determine fire impacts to resources. The effects were many, and they were detailed in the Umpqua's *Wildfire Effects Evaluation Report* (2003).

One effect was to kill about 500 million board feet of merchantable timber. Because the fires burnt in a mosaic across the landscape, fire intensity varied. Past land-use decisions had limited timber-harvest opportunities, and consequently, I elected to focus potential timber salvage sales in areas dedicated to commercial timber production, called "matrix" areas. My decision was also guided by the desire to make the most effective use of the limited funds I had available for environmental analysis and timber sales.

During the worst weather of the 2002 fire season, an arsonist set the Apple Fire on the North Umpqua Ranger District. This fire eventually burned about 18,000 acres of both mature timber and second-growth plantations. Most of the area was matrix and available for commercial timber harvest. The District Ranger, Carol Cushing, elected to offer blackened, dead timber from the matrix area for harvest and proposed to develop an environmental impact statement and decision. Our intent was that the sale if this timber would help pay for part of recovery, including reforestation and stream restoration.

We conducted intense public involvement for all of the salvage timber sales, including Apple. In a larger context, we also explored the sufficiency of the Northwest Forest Plan with regard to large-scale wildfire and found that it came up wanting in many respects.

We held a disturbance-ecology conference in Roseburg in the spring of 2003 to explore how the Northwest Forest Plan dealt with fire, insects, and disease at large scales. I used local and regional experts, as well as nationally known experts such as Chief Emeritus Jack Ward Thomas and Dr. Gordon Reeves (both of whom had helped write the Northwest Forest Plan), and Dr. Daniel Botkin, who wrote *Discordant Harmonies*, a landmark text on ecosystem function and disturbance processes.

Ignored by the Pacific Norwest Regional office and the Rogue-Siskiyou National Forest (the site of the notorious Biscuit Fires that had burned concurrently with the Umpqua fires), the Umpqua Disturbance Ecology Conference concluded that the Northwest Forest Plan was insufficient when it came to large-scale ecological disturbance phenomena. Thus, the Plan's assumptions about long-term ecological conditions and health and habitat protections through conservation area set-asides were thrown into significant doubt. The later Dr. John Sessions report on the Biscuit Fire underscored many of the concerns and conclusions shared at the Umpqua conference and in the Umpqua *Wildfire Effects Evaluation Report*.

The 2003 Disturbance-Ecology Conference had included a significant public involvement component. Individuals and interest groups had participated throughout. One of the conclusions of small-group dialogues, offered by a board member of the Douglas Timber Operators (the local advocacy group for timber and economic development), was to keep meeting to explore the middle ground and new understandings developed at the conference.

In response, we held three further meetings, but we made little progress as each interest preferred to restate established positions rather than work towards collaborative agreements. Still, all participants in the disturbance conference and in the follow-up meetings understood that the conference had shifted the value and influence of the Northwest Forest Plan because some of the Plan's underlying assumptions were incorrect.

As the work on the Apple Fire environmental analysis and decision moved forward, several key issues emerged: logging effects on soils (particularly disturbance and compaction), desire for timber for local mills, timeliness of timber delivery (dead trees lose value as timber the longer they stand on the stump), the number of dead standing trees (snags) to leave on logged sites for wildlife purposes, the amount of large woody debris (downed, dead trees) to leave on the site, and the potential that timber salvage would somehow satisfy the arsonist and encourage future arson.

The planning team and District Ranger Cushing dealt with these issues skillfully, searching for consent to proceed with the salvage effort. At the end of their effort, only two issues remained fundamentally unresolved: the number of snags per acre to be retained and the amount of large woody debris to leave for wildlife purposes on logged sites. Because there had not been an adequate collaborative, community-based, values discussion and agreement, Ranger Cushing issued her decision without having reached consent with all parties.

A full-blown conflict erupted. Environmental groups pursued appeals based on the wide range of issues. Eventually, Cascadia Wildlands Project, the Oregon Natural Resource Coalition, and Umpqua Watersheds, a local environmental group, filed a lawsuit. After discussion, it appeared that the litigating groups opposed salvage timber harvest simply because it was "wrong". These included the key issues that had not been resolved through environmental analysis and public involvement.

At this point, we had structural, compositional, and functional or relationship components in a full-blown conflict. The structural components included concerns that the Apple Fires area was not ecologically capable of withstanding salvage logging and subsequent recovery efforts, and, further, that laws and regulations would not support salvage. We had compositional components that included formal public communications from both development and environmental interests that rejected Ranger Cushing's decision, values-based questions lingering about all key issues, and concerns about cost, timeliness, and target accomplishment from Forest Service leaders. Functional and relationship components included internal questions similar to the external questions about whether salvage logging had ecological merit, and there was deep mistrust among interests and advocates representing environmental and development groups, elected officials, and other agencies.

Although the hard work by Ranger Cushing and her staff had kept the structural, compositional, and relationship components of the conflict from becoming overly complex, thus avoiding "wicked problem" status, we were still in court and our offer of deteriorating timber for sale was delayed. In response to motions, the Court ordered a "mediation," which is actually better described as a "court-ordered, facilitated negotiation" to attempt to resolve the conflict.

It was partially successful. Over an afternoon, the negotiation moved through a step-wise discussion and resolution of issues to an unbridled "horse-trade" of acres and mitigations. With the facilitator's assistance, we resolved the lawsuit in a little over six hours, giving up a portion of the potential timber sale volume.

Apple Fire sales and recovery went forward. The court-initiated facilitated negotiation was effective in conflict resolution short of crisis.

However, we did not address the structural components because there was never a ruling on the merits of the allegations and the elements of the lawsuit. The compositional components changed somewhat because the specific issues of the Apple Fire conflict were set aside in favor of the negotiated settlement with its legal (now structural) requirements. The functional and relationship components changed slightly because environmental interests found that the Umpqua National Forest representatives were capable negotiators who did not bear grudges in later contacts and decisions, because the timber industry saw that the employees remained steadfast in their desire to produce salvage timber, and because elected officials and others saw that the parties to the conflict could reach swift resolution.

Crisis Control along the Scandal Pathway

Pathway Stage	Distress	Scandal	Anarchy	Catastrophe
Issue	Structure	Structure	Structure	Structure
	Composition	Composition	Composition	Composition
	Function/Rela.	Function/Rela.	Function/Rela.	Function/Rela.
Full-blown Conflict	Structure	Structure	Structure	Structure
	Composition	Composition	Composition	Composition
	Function/Rela.	Function/Rela.	Function/Rela.	Function/Rela.
Crisis	Structure	Structure	Structure	Structure
	Composition	Composition	Composition	Composition
	Function/Rela.	Function/Rela.	Function/Rela.	Function/Rela.
Recovery	Structure	Structure	Structure	Structure
	Composition	Composition	Composition	Composition
	Function/Rela.	Function/Rela.	Function/Rela.	Function/Rela.

In one sense, the fundamental difference between a full-blown conflict and a crisis is that, when a crisis happens, the disputants caught up in the conflict can no longer collaboratively resolve the conflict. Therefore, it is not just enough that the crisis is a "watershed" incident that irrevocably changes significant aspects of the structure, composition, and relationships of the dispute; it is also that the change is largely outside the combined control of the parties to the conflict.

As George Bernard Shaw said, *"If you can't get rid of the skeleton in your closet, you'd best teach it to dance."* During a crisis, once the "skeleton" is out of the closet, incidents and outcomes will be out of disputants' control. Others, like the media, will cause the "skeleton to dance."

When the plaintiffs brought the Apple Fire lawsuit, they were hoping to trigger a crisis through the courts that would be favorable to their interests (no logging of burned timber), forcing the Forest Service and the timber industry into a new "watershed" not of their choosing. Because the Forest Service wins the majority of the cases brought against it, and because Umpqua National Forest staff had carefully designed the environmental analysis and decision to be legally sustainable, the plaintiffs' had perhaps a 30% likelihood of success.

That the plaintiffs would achieve everything they wanted was highly unlikely because, in cases like these, the courts often employ some form of "Solomon's rule" in settling the case. The facilitated negotiation brought control over the outcome back to the disputing parties and avoided significant harm to one party or another's interests.

In 2003, a crisis occurred to a business in Roseburg, Oregon that illustrates crisis control very nicely[6]. First Strike, Inc. provides fire-fighting and emergency-response crews nationwide. Some of their employees were returning from a fire assignment in Idaho when one of their vans ran head on into a semi-truck and everyone in the van was killed. The van had been traveling in the wrong lane on a blind curve after crossing a double-yellow line to get there. Early toxicology reports and eyewitness accounts indicated that the van's driver might have been drinking alcohol.

As a community of place, Roseburg was devastated, particularly friends, family, and the local wildland firefighters (of which there are many). Local firefighters, including Forest Service, Bureau of Land Management, and Douglas Forest Protection Association units, helped plan and coordinate a community-wide mourning incident at the Douglas County Fairgrounds. Communities of interest and of fate in the form of firefighters from other communities also expressed their sympathy and showed up. Hundreds of people attended.

It was shortly after the memorial incident that the news broke about the van driver's possible alcohol use and that the prosecutor in the eastern Oregon community where the crash occurred was going to indict the owners of First Strike for criminal negligence. First Strike owners were on the edge of a watershed incident, the recovery from which could include loss of their business or even criminal penalties. They could face years of expensive litigation before recovery could begin.

The First Strike owners were competent and thoughtful people, and they immediately initiated crisis control measures. In fact, without thinking about such a specific, horrific crisis in advance, these measures had begun years before the collision or the filing of criminal charges.

Many years before, the First Strike owners had dedicated themselves to the safety and development of their young firefighters and other employees. The owners had strong safety policies in place and backed them up with action. They could stand before anyone and forthrightly declare their commitment and dedication to safety. They knew with conviction that, whatever the evidence or conclusions of investigations into the accident, their commitment to safety had been, and would continue to be, of the highest order.

---

[6] The information concerning First Strike, Inc. comes from a series of articles in *The News Review,* the local Roseburg paper: "Eight Oregon firefighters killed in van-truck collision" by Rebecca Boone, August 23, 2003; "First Strike safety record is solid" by Christian Bringhurst, August 27, 2003; "First Strike alters driver policy" by John Sowell, September 5, 2003; "Fallen, but not forgotten" by John Sowell, September 7, 2003; "First Strike response to tragedy commendable" editorial, October 12, 2003; "First Strike Aftermath Timeline" November 23, 2003; "Workers given chance at First Strike to earn trust, responsibility" by John Sowell, November 24, 2003; "First Strike charges heading to trial" by John Sowell, February 5, 2004; "First Strike criminal charges dismissed" by John Sowell, February 19, 2004; "Families Relieved" by John Sowell, February 23, 2004; "The learning curves" by John Sowell, March 21, 2004; "Aftermath of First Strike crash brought changes to the industry" by John Sowell, August 24, 2004; and "First Strike tragedy led to needed changes" *News-Review* Editorial, August 19, 2004.

They also never tried to deflect or sidestep their responsibilities, but rather, they took the position publicly that they would abide by the conclusions of the court. They also led the effort to hold the community-wide memorial service. People in the community and interested people throughout Oregon understood their honest acceptance of appropriate responsibility and admired them for it.

They hired highly competent legal counsel and, months later, the prosecutor dropped all charges. He said, "I am satisfied that First Strike has shown that they intend to make changes that will further safeguard their employees and the traveling public. They are so committed to safety that I know they will follow through."

First Strike made several changes, the most significant of which was to send a driver to bring returning crews home. By incurring this considerable expense, the owners assured that a fresh, unhurried driver could bring exhausted, often-sick crews home with little or no danger to themselves or others.

This was a "watershed incident" for First Strike. However, by using effective control measures, they had little unacceptable change imposed upon them. In fact, they continued to hold the public's respect and admiration. They emerged as industry leaders in the area of crew safety.

In First Strike's case, conflict structure did not change during the crisis. **They used compositional factors and actions (effective crisis communications, including the memorial service, and driver policies) to effect threatening structural changes (criminal charges and possible business loss)**. Moreover, even while they were mourning their losses, which they felt deeply, the owners were building relationships in the community and state-wide. Scandal crisis controlled!

Recovery along the Scandal Pathway

Pathway / Stage	Distress	Scandal	Anarchy	Catastrophe
Issue	Structure	Structure	Structure	Structure
	Composition	Composition	Composition	Composition
	Function/Rela.	Function/Rela.	Function/Rela.	Function/Rela.
Full-blown Conflict	Structure	Structure	Structure	Structure
	Composition	Composition	Composition	Composition
	Function/Rela.	Function/Rela.	Function/Rela.	Function/Rela.
Crisis	Structure	Structure	Structure	Structure
	Composition	Composition	Composition	Composition
	Function/Rela.	Function/Rela.	Function/Rela.	Function/Rela.
Recovery	Structure	Structure	Structure	Structure
	Composition	Composition	Composition	Composition
	Function/Rela.	Function/Rela.	Function/Rela.	Function/Rela.

By controlling their crisis, First Strike was well on their way to recovery when the crisis ended. They avoided the long period of blaming that often follows a crisis. To the extent they could, they participated in and remained in charge of the changes imposed and could sustain their leadership and organization. They settled the issues of guilt and liability quickly and thus could work on healing their personal lives and internal relationships. They are an excellent example of effective crisis control leading to a prompt recovery.

If we look back on the Watergate scandal, we see a much longer, more difficult, and possibly still-continuing recovery. President Nixon resigned. His Vice-President, Gerald Ford, pardoned him — there is little talk about it now but this is one of the more significant recovery-through-reconciliation acts in American history. Many of the President's advisors and the Watergate "plumbers" were convicted of various crimes and served prison sentences (they were not pardoned).

Recovery took at least a decade, and in some respects, we have not fully recovered after 30 years. Some of the President's counselors made radical changes in their lives, becoming pastors and pacifists, but others, such as G. Gordon Liddy, remained unrepentant.

Issues about executive privilege, campaign finance, and political "dirty tricks" remain unresolved and continue.

As a significant scandal, "Watergate" is still a watchword. In fact, more recent national, political scandals sometimes have "-gate" added to the end of their title in acknowledgement of the iconic nature of Watergate. Remember "Iran-gate" and the "arms-for-hostages" scandal during the Reagan Administration and "travel-gate" during the Clinton Presidency?

In the case of Watergate and the other "-gates" that followed, the compositional and relationship changes were immediate and relatively clear. Congress, the Courts, and public interest groups are still tinkering with the structural components, such a campaign security and finance issues.

Chapter 4: Travel along the Anarchy Pathway

Dispute Pathology: each dispute displays a unique pathology in the form of structural, compositional, and functional or relationship elements; depending on these elements, disputes can be understood as distress, scandal, <u>anarchy</u>, or catastrophe pathways; disputes vary in intensity and complexity from issues to full-blown conflict, to crisis and to recovery; for many disputes, unacceptable losses seem to appear as full-blown conflicts emerge.

Pathway Stage	Distress	Scandal	Anarchy	Catastrophe
Issue	Structure	Structure	Structure	Structure
	Composition	Composition	Composition	Composition
	Function/Rela.	Function/Rela.	Function/Rela.	Function/Rela.
Full-blown Conflict	Structure	Structure	Structure	Structure
	Composition	Composition	Composition	Composition
	Function/Rela.	Function/Rela.	Function/Rela.	Function/Rela.
Crisis	Structure	Structure	Structure	Structure
	Composition	Composition	Composition	Composition
	Function/Rela.	Function/Rela.	Function/Rela.	Function/Rela.
Recovery	Structure	Structure	Structure	Structure
	Composition	Composition	Composition	Composition
	Function/Rela.	Function/Rela.	Function/Rela.	Function/Rela.

This chapter covers the journey down the anarchy pathway. Anarchy refers to an attempt by a person or group to overcome laws, regulations, rules, ethics, or societal norms in order to impose a significantly modified or new order. This new status usually represents the values of a minority or recent minority-turned-majority.

Anarchy assumes that a transition period, perhaps exhibiting lawlessness, may occur during the transition to the new status quo. Anarchy-related communications often contain accusations of authoritarian decadence or apathy, abuses of authority and reprisal or repression, and discrimination against minority interests or the "powerless."

At times, the Forest Service, Bureau of Land Management, and other state and local agencies deal with anarchist tree sitters, demonstrators, or other protestors. The communications from the protestors to society-at-large often take the form of messages about a small, embattled minority of caring people forced by the actions of the Forest Service to sacrifice their time and comfort, and perhaps their lives, to protect vanishing resources. Scandal-mongering statements about how the Forest service is "acting outside the law" may also accompany these anarchistic messages. "Direct" anarchistic actions, like tree sitting and tree spiking, often accompany legal or media actions that are at the same time mechanisms for crying scandal.

Occasionally, anarchists will take hostages as a means to project their power and gain attention for their cause. "Hostages" can be people, natural resources, structures, or equipment. Hostage taking can also target a single individual, general or specific groups, or more rarely, work sites or even whole towns or communities (by blocking transportation routes or other access). For anarchists, hostages constitute a tactical advantage, giving the anarchists media attention, protection from assault or reprisal, and a bargaining chip to ask for concessions or change.

Human hostages sometimes experience the "Stockholm syndrome," which is a form of resistance psychology: to save their lives and preserve their health, the hostages "join" the anarchists' cause, at least until the hostages gain freedom. In some cases, the hostage support for the anarchists extends beyond release. The "Stockholm" experience stemmed from a Swedish bank robbery in which some of the hostages defended the robbers and later went to court to testify on their behalf. Patty Hearst was a famous victim of the syndrome when she was in the hands of the Symbionese Liberation Army, a 1960s urban anarchy group — she assisted them in bank robbery and violent acts some months after her kidnapping.

America has institutionalized anarchy to create beneficial change, avoiding lawlessness for the most part. Anarchy can create autonomy for minority interests, or it can overthrow the established power structures and elites. The Boston Tea Party was anarchy attached to a property crime, and it led to the birth of a great democratic nation. The election of the Republican Congress in 1994 and the Democratic Congress of 2008 were anarchic because the elections imposed the will of America's active voters on an established social order and power structure. The elections were also followed by peaceful transfers of power in the best traditions of the U.S.

Therefore, anarchists propose to impose a new order that represents different values without necessarily eliminating government or social order. **Anarchy can in fact be evolutionary**, as in the orderly change of power from one elected administration to another. **Anarchy can be revolutionary, too**, as in the Bolshevik Revolution that imposed a minority communist totalitarian regime over a majority post-czarist regime. In the classic sense, anarchists can also seek to create conditions without government, or with minimal "gangster" government, as in the breakdown of social order and government in places like Haiti and the Sudan over the past several years.

Anarchy is different from "nihilism," which is the desire to reject and destroy all vestiges of traditional morality, government, and social control. The Pol Pot regime in Cambodia in the 1970s showed signs of nihilistic philosophy, purportedly placing politically indoctrinated children in charge of social development and the elimination of dissenters.

Often their disputants refer to anarchists in nihilistic terms, such as "outlaws," "lawless" or "lawbreakers," "bomb throwers," or "revolutionaries." Anarchists' supporters may refer to them as "freedom fighters," "revolutionaries," "counter-revolutionaries," "heroes," "martyrs," or "change agents."

The phrase that describes the action of anarchy and communications is "promoting (or fomenting) anarchy." The person taking the action is an "anarchist." The anarchist focuses on exposing social inequity, abuse of authority, and decadent or anti-social behaviors by the ruling elites.

Like other disputes, anarchy represents values conflicts and concerns power and control. Also like scandal, anarchies may be characterized as either "effective" or "ineffective," depending on whether they actually change behaviors or exert control over incidents.

Anarchists may be of any political philosophy. Conservative anarchists tend to focus on traditional values and conditions they would like to see continued or reinstated. Liberal or progressive anarchists tend to focus on utopian or emerging values and conditions that replace traditional values.

The American revolutionary leaders of 1776 were unusual in that they espoused emerging political values but came from the wealthy middle class of colonists. The new order they imposed reflects an emphasis on peace and justice to create the maximum potential for "happiness," which they understood meant both the ownership of property and the exercise of individual rights guaranteeing freedom.

Issues Abatement along the Anarchy Pathway

Pathway Stage	Distress	Scandal	Anarchy	Catastrophe
Issue	Structure	Structure	Structure	Structure
	Composition	Composition	Composition	Composition
	Function/Rela.	Function/Rela.	Function/Rela.	Function/Rela.
Full-blown Conflict	Structure	Structure	Structure	Structure
	Composition	Composition	Composition	Composition
	Function/Rela.	Function/Rela.	Function/Rela.	Function/Rela.
Crisis	Structure	Structure	Structure	Structure
	Composition	Composition	Composition	Composition
	Function/Rela.	Function/Rela.	Function/Rela.	Function/Rela.
Recovery	Structure	Structure	Structure	Structure
	Composition	Composition	Composition	Composition
	Function/Rela.	Function/Rela.	Function/Rela.	Function/Rela.

Anarchy often presents itself first as a protest against the status quo, whether laws, regulations, social norms or land-management decisions. Conservative or reactionary anarchists often base their protests on "states' rights," Constitutional, or Biblical grounds. Progressive or utopian anarchists often base their protests on a failure to achieve ideals or to respond to the latest scientific or other information about resource conditions, capabilities, and trends. Both groups tend to offer their protests as a comparison of current conditions against desired future conditions, however socially retrogressive or progressive. In EDR work, sorting out what types are present and what specific protests exist is quite important.

The anarchist's thoughts and positions are important, of course, but so also are the thoughts and positions of the target individuals, agencies, or a small group. Sometimes, the media or uninvolved-but-interested third parties are also useful as well, particularly to help define the key issues raised and their relative importance.

When I arrived as Forest Supervisor on the Umpqua National Forest in 2002, an environmental analysis of grazing activities on the Tiller Ranger District had been ongoing since 1997. A decision was long overdue, but good reasons existed for why a conclusion remained elusive.

Environmentalists held that livestock grazing had to conform to existing laws, regulations, and directions from the courts and the Northwest Forest Plan, and the Forest Service agreed with this viewpoint. To go forward at all, we had to regulate the grazing program and the livestock grazers according to the law. We also had an Umpqua National Forest guiding principle about protecting traditional cultures, like the stockmen, and supporting people who wanted to live a rural lifestyle. Environmentalists also held out certain additional expectations but were generally non-specific about them, neither crying scandal nor pursuing anarchy over the time of my involvement with the decision.

Grazers, particularly a local, conservative rancher, held that grazing should return to past patterns and stocking levels. According to his values, regulations should simply say, "Turn 'em out in the spring and pick 'em up in the fall. The stragglers will wander home when the snow drives 'em down." One of the first fieldtrips I went on as a new Forest Supervisor was with him, and we drove around the District most of the day discussing the issues with the resources right in front of us. At the end of the day, we respected one another; and later, we became friends.

On that day, and in later meetings, it was also clear to me that the requirements we faced under the law confused him and he hoped to find some means, legal or political, to return the livestock program to past practices and conditions. He was frustrated, and he frequently mentioned his impulse to act against the law, saying things like, "What would you do if I just turned out 300 head and let them follow the snow to the high ground?" He also looked for old federal laws that would trump the current laws, plans, and court rulings. He questioned the assumptions about resource conditions and effects in the environmental analysis. Based on years of resource observation that generations of his family had made in the area, he wanted the retrograde option — an option that was not available to me.

He was a fine citizen and a dedicated community leader, a patriot and a businessperson who wanted good things for his community. He was merely frustrated and impatient with a government that seemed focused on meeting environmental goals in his backyard, goals that seemed contrary to local interests. He was also a non-violent anarchist trying to overthrow the established order in the finest American tradition.

The many years' delay in reaching a conclusion allowed local Forest Service employees to work out many of his issues while field testing and monitoring trial grazing practices to assure regulations and appropriate resource conditions were met. Early in 2006, I signed the Record of Decision for a Final Environmental Impact Statement, allowing him and his fellow livestock grazers to turn out greater numbers of cattle than they had been able to do for many years. They could not "turn out 300 head in the spring and pick 'em up in the fall," but by following certain practices, they could get back on the transitional range that we could offer up on the forest and continue to pursue their rural lifestyle.

In this case, we kept the dispute limited to a few issues. The numbers of participants remained few, with most of the dispute focused on the rancher who opposed agency policies. Communications were relatively easy because the numbers of participants and interested onlookers permitted limited communications channels and messages. My decision was not appealed or litigated.

Resolving Full-Blown Conflict along the Anarchy Pathway

Pathway / Stage	Distress	Scandal	Anarchy	Catastrophe
Issue	Structure	Structure	Structure	Structure
	Composition	Composition	Composition	Composition
	Function/Rela.	Function/Rela.	Function/Rela.	Function/Rela.
Full-blown Conflict	Structure	Structure	Structure	Structure
	Composition	Composition	Composition	Composition
	Function/Rela.	Function/Rela.	Function/Rela.	Function/Rela.
Crisis	Structure	Structure	Structure	Structure
	Composition	Composition	Composition	Composition
	Function/Rela.	Function/Rela.	Function/Rela.	Function/Rela.
Recovery	Structure	Structure	Structure	Structure
	Composition	Composition	Composition	Composition
	Function/Rela.	Function/Rela.	Function/Rela.	Function/Rela.

If we had not managed the dispute at the issues level, we might have faced escalation to a full-blown conflict. Catron County, NM and Nye County, NV have both hosted full-blown conflicts over grazing. Conservative anarchists in these locales have opposed government actions or inaction, and others, such as environmentalists and elected officials, have also weighed in. These conflicts have evolved into crises from time to time, and violence has punctuated some of the conflicts, including bombings of Forest Service property and a District Ranger's personal vehicle.

The worst domestic terror incident in modern U.S. history was conservative anarchist Timothy McVey's bombing of the Murrah Federal Building in Oklahoma City. This bombing occurred during a low-key full-blown conflict over government handling of the Waco and Ruby Ridge incidents. Although debates over the incidents were ongoing, the nation as a whole was not in the midst of a crisis about these incidents at the time of the McVey bombing; however, conservative anarchists were in an uproar within their own circles. The bombing did not permanently alter major structural, compositional, or relationship factors, and so it did not trigger a crisis. Treated as criminals, McVey and his accomplice met justice.

While in Alaska as Acting Regional Forester for 18 months, I dealt with a full-blown conflict over a recreational outfitter. His permit was for river fishing and guiding in a small rural Alaskan town. For a number of years, he had been cheating on his payments under his permit, reporting fewer clients than he actually served. The permittee was wealthy, and he had excellent political contacts both in Alaska and across the nation because of the wealthy, out-of-state clients he served.

Forest Service law enforcement, under the leadership of the Department of Justice, had developed a clear case against the permittee with witness statements and videotapes. The Attorney General charged him with twelve felony violations of federal law.

At this point, options to conclude the case were easily available. One option was for the permittee to give up the permit, either voluntarily or through agency revocation. Another option was for the permittee to come into compliance with the permit, pay back-fees, accept a criminal penalty (it was his second, willful offense), and accept a one-year extension on his permit while he showed good faith at following the rules.

The outfitter chose to escalate the dispute into a full-blown conflict.

He threw the town into an uproar over the situation, trying to get local people to bring pressure to bear on the District Ranger and staff. Next, his attorney attacked the basis for the Forest Service' enforcement, claiming that the agency lacked jurisdiction on state highways and waterways. The Forest Service authority extends from the "property clause" of the Constitution, and the courts support such enforcements. I did not want this petty criminal case to escalate to a Constitutional question, but the permittee pursued this conservative anarchist approach.

In support of his position, the permittee also activated his extensive local and national networks and raised a ruckus. He got the state legislature to pass a resolution condemning the Forest Service for violating Alaska sovereignty regarding the highways over which he transported his gear. He got the Governor's Office to attack the Forest Service for violating Alaska sovereignty regarding waterways over which he transported his boats and clients. Ultimately, he got Alaska's Department of Fish and Wildlife employees to offer statements to the court condemning the Forest Service and articulating arcane legal theories about state sovereignty.

The Fish and Wildlife employees contacted the Executive Director of the International Association of Fish and Wildlife Agencies and Forest Service Chief Emeritus, Max Peterson, to recruit me to attack the federal Constitutional "property clause" case. Late in the conflict, the Clinton Administration left office and the George W. Bush

Administration came in. The new Administration added pressure on the Department of Justice to settle the case.

The numbers of issues and participants expanded rapidly. Rapid accumulation of political and social pressure also occurred. Communications got quite complicated as the issues escalated into a full-blown state-wide and national-scale conflict. Because the case involved a criminal proceeding, Forest Service employees could not comment publicly about the case or the permittee, but his communications could be unrestrained. Crisis in the form of Congressional action over agency administration of recreational permits loomed on the horizon.

I knew that the permittee's escalation had happened quickly and people were confused about the facts and about applications of law. I knew that the nature of the case, particularly the criminal aspects, would keep elected officials focused on the broader sovereignty issues because the courts and the public take a dim view of political meddling in criminal prosecutions. I wanted to act before anarchic public opinions consolidated and pressures mounted to the point where other interests intervened and we became gridlocked.

I also knew that the Forest Service could not abandon our mandate to enforce the Constitution or the laws Congress passed in compliance with the Constitution.

Through informal communications and attorney-to-attorney contact, I knew that the permittee was afraid of losing his permit — **this was his core issue**. Therefore, I asked the Department of Justice attorneys **to drop the permit-loss option**. A few weeks later, the permittee agreed to the option that protected his permit and admitted his guilt to two felonies before the court. The full-blown conflict collapsed and was resolved short of crisis.

Crisis Control along the Anarchy Pathway

Pathway Stage	Distress	Scandal	Anarchy	Catastrophe
Issue	Structure	Structure	Structure	Structure
	Composition	Composition	Composition	Composition
	Function/Rela.	Function/Rela.	Function/Rela.	Function/Rela.
Full-blown Conflict	Structure	Structure	Structure	Structure
	Composition	Composition	Composition	Composition
	Function/Rela.	Function/Rela.	Function/Rela.	Function/Rela.
Crisis	Structure	Structure	Structure	Structure
	Composition	Composition	Composition	Composition
	Function/Rela.	Function/Rela.	Function/Rela.	Function/Rela.
Recovery	Structure	Structure	Structure	Structure
	Composition	Composition	Composition	Composition
	Function/Rela.	Function/Rela.	Function/Rela.	Function/Rela.

I stated this previously in other parts of this book and the companion Theory and Principles book: the fundamental difference between a full-blown conflict and a crisis is that, when a crisis happens, the disputants caught up in the conflict can no longer collaboratively resolve the conflict. Resolution is out of their hands. Therefore, it is not just enough that the crisis is a "watershed" incident that irrevocably changes significant aspects of the structure, composition, and relationships of the dispute; it is also that the change is largely outside the combined control of the disputants.

What would have happened if the permittee and I had failed to communicate effectively to resolve the conflict? The permittee could easily have lost his permit and paid large fines or even served jail time. In response to this and other perceived cases of abused authority, Congress could have passed legislation limiting our authority to have or enforce permits. Most critically, with the outfitter out of business, the public could have lost a great recreational opportunity in a remote Alaskan village that depends on tourism for its existence.

As mentioned previously in Chapter 9, I had an earlier incident to motivate my actions. When I arrived in Alaska in 1996 as Deputy Regional Forester for Natural Resources, I was well aware of past tensions between the state of Alaska and the federal government over sovereignty issues. In fact, I had a personal list of four structural and compositional changes I wanted to institute to lessen the potential for disputes in the future.

One of the items on my list concerned years of inter-agency clashes over enforcement of Alaska Title 16, a statute that asserts state authority over fish and wildlife resources on federal lands. Like other states, Alaska's authority to regulate fish and wildlife on federal land rests on informal traditional agreements, which are compositional and relationship elements, and not on an explicit structural base like a federal law. Therefore, when federal employees chose to ignore Alaska Fish and Game employees, often when personalities clashed or professionals disagreed, state employees were understandably frustrated and angry.

Just before I had arrived in 1996, District Ranger Joe Chiarella of the Hoonah District of the Chatham Area, Tongass National Forest was attempting to replace a malfunctioning culvert. The culvert was on private land, but it was subject to Joe's authority because of a federal easement permitting access for a logging road and other purposes.

Accompanied by an armed federal law enforcement officer when they went out to work on the culvert, Joe and his crew had heard that the state might send a trooper to arrest them. The state's justification for the potential arrests rested on Alaska Title 16 authority for the state to control activities like culvert replacement because they affected anadromous and resident fish stocks. Under federal law, the trooper was subject to arrest if he interfered with federal officials trying to perform their duties. The situation was more complicated because the federal culvert was on private land under the provisions of an easement, making jurisdictions even murkier than if the culvert had been on federal land.

The armed confrontation ensued, but, thanks to the professionalism of the people present, no guns were drawn and no arrests made. Even so, a full-blown conflict had reached early crisis stage—one tinged with the potential for violence.

After discussions with Fred Norbury, Regional Planning and Budget Director, I asked that he and his staff negotiate a written agreement with Alaska to de-escalate the early crisis. They did this capably over the next year or so, and we were able to establish a cooperative relationship based mainly on information exchanges at the right times, codified in an enforceable written agreement. This agreement among governments was a structural change put in place to explicitly acknowledge and respect both Alaska and federal authorities and deescalate the conflict to more easily managed issues.

State leaders and I had imposed the permanent changes. Displeased by the changes, field employees in both agencies had to deal with new work requirements with timelines and accountability. **Disputant displeasure is a common outcome of controlled crisis because the permanent changes occurred out of the control of the disputing parties and they did not like the result**.

To borrow a cigarette-advertising motto: "the field staff would have rather fought than switched," but switch they did before things got truly bad!

Recovery Along the Anarchy Pathway

Pathway / Stage	Distress	Scandal	Anarchy	Catastrophe
Issue	Structure	Structure	Structure	Structure
	Composition	Composition	Composition	Composition
	Function/Rela.	Function/Rela.	Function/Rela.	Function/Rela.
Full-blown Conflict	Structure	Structure	Structure	Structure
	Composition	Composition	Composition	Composition
	Function/Rela.	Function/Rela.	Function/Rela.	Function/Rela.
Crisis	Structure	Structure	Structure	Structure
	Composition	Composition	Composition	Composition
	Function/Rela.	Function/Rela.	Function/Rela.	Function/Rela.
Recovery	Structure	Structure	Structure	Structure
	Composition	Composition	Composition	Composition
	Function/Rela.	Function/Rela.	Function/Rela.	Function/Rela.

If anarchy is effective, recovery displays behavior that tests the new structure, composition, and relationships, particularly concerning power and control. New coalitions form to define the new status quo and to divide power and authority. Recovery may display less blaming than scandal recovery because the focus is on defining new power relationships.

If anarchy is ineffective, recovery looks somewhat like scandal recovery. New coalitions may be forming and power may be shared differently, but the changes are limited and the fundamental dispute may still be intact and capable of generating more conflict and a similar crisis. Blaming along the lines of previously existing communications and positions may be common.

For example, the Monongahela Controversy in the 1970s was an example of effective anarchy. The Monongahela Controversy concerned the clear cutting of a favorite squirrel hunting area in West Virginia. Hunters protested, challenged federal authority for harvesting live trees, and advocated for change. They were successful and a new order emerged when Congress passed the Forest and Rangeland Renewable Resources Planning Act, the National Forest Management Act, and other legislation to define public lands management more clearly and precisely.

Along with Wilderness Acts, the Federal Land Planning and Management Act, and the Endangered Species Act, the effect of this body of legislation created direction for many agencies into the future, and these acts established a pattern of legislation regarding public lands and natural resources that was historically unprecedented in scope and intensity. Triggered by the hunters on the Monongahela National Forest, the anarchy eventually involved federal courts to the Supreme Court level, Congress, natural resource interest groups of every kind, public officials, and thousands of employees and common citizens. Every American felt the effects, and the legislation affected thinking about natural resources worldwide.

Since the passage of the National Forest Management Act and other related legislation, the Forest Service, the courts, interest groups, and agency partners have been sorting out structural, compositional, and relationship factors implied within the acts. What do the laws mean? What authorities, real or perceived, exist under the laws? How do the acts enable or restrict land and resource management? Answers to these and hundreds of other questions helped define the power of the many agencies and interests involved.

Chapter 5: Travel along the Catastrophe Pathway

Dispute Pathology: each dispute displays a unique pathology in the form of structural, compositional, and functional or relationship elements; depending on these elements, disputes can be understood as distress, scandal, anarchy, or <u>catastrophe</u> pathways; disputes vary in intensity and complexity from issues to full-blown conflict, to crisis and to recovery; for many disputes, unacceptable losses seem to appear as full-blown conflicts emerge.

Pathway / Stage	Distress	Scandal	Anarchy	Catastrophe
Issue	Structure	Structure	Structure	Structure
	Composition	Composition	Composition	Composition
	Function/Rela.	Function/Rela.	Function/Rela.	Function/Rela.
Full-blown Conflict	Structure	Structure	Structure	Structure
	Composition	Composition	Composition	Composition
	Function/Rela.	Function/Rela.	Function/Rela.	Function/Rela.
Crisis	Structure	Structure	Structure	Structure
	Composition	Composition	Composition	Composition
	Function/Rela.	Function/Rela.	Function/Rela.	Function/Rela.
Recovery	Structure	Structure	Structure	Structure
	Composition	Composition	Composition	Composition
	Function/Rela.	Function/Rela.	Function/Rela.	Function/Rela.

This chapter covers the journey down the catastrophe pathway. This pathway is significantly different from the other three because this pathway is **much less about inter-personal or societal disputes than it is about unacceptable losses imposed on people and the human environment** from natural or human-infrastructure-caused incidents or "incidents" as they are called by emergency managers. Of course, a host of related human disputes can cascade from catastrophes.

Regarding catastrophes, "unacceptable losses" can mean many things, but for natural incidents along the catastrophe pathway, the term refers to impacts and conditions outside the range of natural variation. For example, a condition might be the accumulation of fuels (e.g., grasses, twigs, branches, entire dead trees) far greater than existed historically. The incident could be a landscape-scale fire that consumed those fuels, and because of the greatly increased fuels and resulting fire intensity, it killed all the trees in a place where such "stand-replacing" fires would not naturally occur.

For human-infrastructure-caused incidents, unacceptable loss refers to disruptions leading to lost quality of life, or of life itself. For example, a dam breaks and homes are washed away, the torrent kills and maims people, and whole communities may require rebuilding.

At the end of the day, whether a catastrophe has occurred or not is a human judgment predicated on people's values and quality of life measures. Another way of saying this is that people measure catastrophes at human scale and people decide whether an incident constitutes a catastrophe or not.

For idea-continuity and consistency purposes, I will use these EDR terms — "dispute," "issue," "conflict," "crisis," and "recovery" — as if nature or human-built infrastructure were animate and capable of entering into a dispute. This "incident-with-a-personality" metaphor is not perfect, but the phenomena and effects are similar enough as regards EDR that I chose to allow for a "dispute" (more a relationship with a certain tension) between a dam and the community of fate that lives below it or a fire and the person who feels the threat and heat from it.

To support my usage, ecology and complexity experts speak to complex natural systems as having apparent purpose and describe system behaviors as if systems had intention. This also may be personification of non-human things but, once again, the descriptions are useful for defining and understanding human relationships to non-human system components.

Society puts considerable energy into trying to forecast potential catastrophes. For example, every morning we look at the weather forecast to help us decide what to wear and whether we need to take protective clothing or an umbrella. Fifty years ago, the daily weather forecast was frequently in error, and weathermen were often mocked and the butt of jokes. Today, mockery about weather-people is rare. With satellite monitoring of weather patterns, Doppler radar to give us a more precise local picture, and computer models to predict weather movements and conditions, the weather forecast is highly reliable on a daily and even weekly basis. Weather experts now provide information that is critical to the daily functions of society, and their reports serve as harbingers of dangerous weather incidents such as tornadoes

Whether we are trying to forecast climate conditions, checking bridge structures to see if they can carry their rated traffic load, or trying to predict wildland fire potential, our focus is on trying to define the threat associated with a given set of conditions or the potential for an incident. We assess the threat by rating and analyzing risk, vulnerability, and potential consequences. Natural resource and dispute managers build scenarios from their analysis of these variables and sometimes test those scenarios with readiness exercises.

In the case of the fuels and fire example, the threat calculation might include risk-assessment studies of the fuels buildup, historic burn intensities and patterns, soil moistures, current and projected weather conditions, and lightening potential. Vulnerability assessments would include proximity of humans and property to the potential intense fire area. Vulnerability could also include assessments of potential losses of habitat to threatened, endangered, or sensitive species, or the potential for the spread of invasive plant species. Managers would then want to estimate potential consequences, such as the loss of people's homes or destruction of built infrastructure like power lines.

During the Mio Fire of 1980, I helped the Forest Service Eastern Region leaders deal with the fire's human consequences. The Mio Fire was a "prescribed" fire set by Forest Service employees to create habitat for the Kirkland's Warbler, an endangered bird species. The prescribed fire was to be 110 acres, but changing wind conditions combined with fuels to result in a nearly 60,000-acre burn. About 55 structures were lost, including homes.

I was able to help the Eastern region leaders by examining the consequences of property loss and looking for the means to confront the looming human-caused fire scandal and personal distress issues. We targeted communications on the affected people and communities. Even while the Mio Fire was still burning, we fielded teams of adjusters to begin the process of compensating people for their losses.

Those measures helped, but the go-head that I sought to work with the deeper issues of post-incident traumatic stress at the community and individual levels was denied, as was my request to rebuild lost trust across the Mio Fire area.

Catastrophic incidents and disputes **often cascade into scandal, anarchy, and distress disputes**. The Mio Fire was my earliest introduction to this phenomenon.

Issues Abatement along the Catastrophe Pathway

Pathway Stage	Distress	Scandal	Anarchy	Catastrophe
Issue	Structure	Structure	Structure	Structure
	Composition	Composition	Composition	Composition
	Function/Rela.	Function/Rela.	Function/Rela.	Function/Rela.
Full-blown Conflict	Structure	Structure	Structure	Structure
	Composition	Composition	Composition	Composition
	Function/Rela.	Function/Rela.	Function/Rela.	Function/Rela.
Crisis	Structure	Structure	Structure	Structure
	Composition	Composition	Composition	Composition
	Function/Rela.	Function/Rela.	Function/Rela.	Function/Rela.
Recovery	Structure	Structure	Structure	Structure
	Composition	Composition	Composition	Composition
	Function/Rela.	Function/Rela.	Function/Rela.	Function/Rela.

Issues related to catastrophe generally concern threat perceptions and response strategy, capacity, and composition. People perceive threat quite differently depending on their experience, knowledge, apparent values-at-risk, and perceived vulnerability.

I have been in many public meetings regarding fire threats to communities and private property. In one case, a homeowner was an outspoken advocate for maximizing property protection by wildland firefighters because he was deep in the woods and surrounded by fuels — he was very angry with the government for threatening his home. His neighbor was allegedly trying to burn his own house down to collect insurance or government compensation (it was too wet and it did not work). A second neighbor had spent a few years clearing brush, saplings, and dead limbs and trees from around his property and had few concerns — he wanted financial assistance made available to more homeowners for fuels-clearing purposes because he had made such good use of it.

The homeowners had three distinctly different threat perceptions. The issues that rose among them included how the government would appraise values if property were lost to fire, who was to blame for the fire situation, how to allocate scarce firefighting personnel and equipment, and frequency and quality of crisis communications. These homeowners were dealing with an actual fire threat burning just a few miles away, an "escaped" fire (another prescribed fire that had jumped its boundaries) headed generally in their direction. Therefore, as I was speaking to the homeowners, we were in a full-blown conflict with a potential crisis looming.

If we had been able to tackle the issues while they were still "young," we would have had a few individuals involved. Many homeowners do not perceive threat until it is imminent. However, a presentation that portrays the structural, compositional, and functional or relationship factors that constitute a threat to their persons or property often convinces people that conditions warrant some planning and preemptive actions.

Structural issues include the physical and biological factors, such as fuels buildup and fire threat. Other structural issues include public firefighting authorities, appropriations for fuels work, preparation, suppression, and authorities for homeowner information and assistance programs. Compositional factors include actual assistance delivery capability for the area, available and complete firefighting and evacuation plans, and the presence of firefighting personnel and equipment. Functional and relationship factors include the quality and nature of neighbor-to-neighbor communications, trust in local officials and firefighting, and the ability of firefighters from many organizations to communicate, cooperate, and collaborate when necessary.

The key to managing catastrophe-related issues is to make an appropriate estimate of the problem or threat, a clear statement of assumptions about risk, vulnerability, and consequences, and an adequate exploration of the range of options available to the participants to respond to the threats.

This contingency planning for threats to individuals, communities, and regions is at the heart of issues abatement. In the context of the plan, practitioners must factually explore the issues and examine them from a personal-values standpoint. They should test the thinking among participants about threat responses thoroughly. The contingency plan itself is a compositional element, and there are key performance and communications values and practices embedded within it.

Resolving Conflict along the Catastrophe Pathway

Pathway Stage	Distress	Scandal	Anarchy	Catastrophe
Issue	Structure	Structure	Structure	Structure
	Composition	Composition	Composition	Composition
	Function/Rela.	Function/Rela.	Function/Rela.	Function/Rela.
Full-blown Conflict	Structure	Structure	Structure	Structure
	Composition	Composition	Composition	Composition
	Function/Rela.	Function/Rela.	Function/Rela.	Function/Rela.
Crisis	Structure	Structure	Structure	Structure
	Composition	Composition	Composition	Composition
	Function/Rela.	Function/Rela.	Function/Rela.	Function/Rela.
Recovery	Structure	Structure	Structure	Structure
	Composition	Composition	Composition	Composition
	Function/Rela.	Function/Rela.	Function/Rela.	Function/Rela.

Once an incident like a fire, earthquake, hurricane, or dam rupture occurs, assumptions in the contingency plan are tested. Dispute escalation to full-blown conflict, or even crisis, may be rapid or it may be slow, but the effect of the incident is to force escalation. Escalation occurs because the structural and compositional factors change, as do the effects on people caught up in the changes.

As contingency and emergency plans roll into action, the importance of training and practice become obvious. Untested emergency systems rarely work exactly as designed and built. Therefore, in the full-blown conflict situation, untested systems may collapse and be ineffective or worse, synergistically exacerbate the catastrophe.

For example, if the smoke from a wildfire reaches a power line and the power line remains "hot," electricity may arc from the line through the moisture in the smoke to the ground. The arcing can trigger more fires, harm firefighters, and ultimately damage or destroy the power line itself. Shutting off power to the lines in the path of a fire is part of contingency planning for a fire situation, and if that remains undone, the potential for fire spread and harm to people and property is greatly increased.

In the process of developing contingency plans, and in the actual response to an "incident" (the word emergency responders use to describe the catastrophic event), people and agencies have to cooperate and collaborate. Lives, property, and protection of natural systems may depend on close cooperation. Yet, the individuals and agencies that have to collaborate often argue over strategy, tactics, staffing, and shared equipment. These disputes sometimes escalate into full-blown conflicts during the incident and crisis, but it is often in the crisis aftermath that the disputants decisively confront their conflicts.

One reason for this is that emergency response authorities usually practice autocratic management. A "fire boss" or "fire incident commander" with extensive training and experience runs the firefighting effort. Because operations deal with emergencies and possible catastrophe, exacting analyses inform, and a strong sense of urgency permeates, operational decisions. The incident commander's decisions have to be consistent with strategy approved by the local agency administrator, but the incident commander runs the day-to-day operations. The operations closely resemble military operations with strong central control, strong radio or telephone communications, and clear chains of command running from incident commanders to active fire-suppression units working on the fire line. If disputes disturb or disrupt this arrangement, the fire may consume lives and property.

In terms of the "nature versus human" conflicts, the effective use of the personnel and equipment available to staff the incident should resolve the conflict short of crisis. If the incident exceeds the ability of the first responders, and additional mobilization has to occur, then the conflict has evolved into a crisis. This certainly happened in the case of the Mio Fire. Additional firefighting resources backed up the fire-use crew that initially set the fire. Once the weather changed and the winds came up, those forces were inadequate and large-scale mobilization occurred, taking control away from the "initial attack" forces, who were ranger district employees.

In terms of the catastrophe-related person-to-person conflicts dealt with after incident-management action, they primarily concern compositional and relationship issues. Occasionally, structural issues, such as who is responsible for the management of an incident, will come up.

In 2002, for example, people confronted me after the fire season about the Timbered Rock Fire that had occurred at the extreme southern end of the Umpqua National Forest, at the point where it conjoined BLM and Rogue National Forest lands. The Timbered Rock Fire was actually three lightning-caused fires that occurred in a cluster.

The Forest Service staffed the fires initially because Forest Service firefighters were close by. Those initial attack forces suppressed two fires. One fire was dangerous and hard to fight because it was located in the bottom of a canyon. Fire leaders placed that fire under observation, and after consulting all local landowners, they delayed active firefighting.

Because of other major fires burning nearby, including the complex of fires on the Umpqua and the Biscuit complex on the Siskiyou, Timbered Rock received no additional resources. Eventually, the weather changed and the fire spread out of the canyon. It burned public lands and resources, and it burned about 12,000 acres of private commercial forest.

The owners of the private forestlands were appropriately angry and blamed the Forest Service for allowing the fire to escape. People attributed that failure to my staff and to me. The critics raised a structural issue concerning who "owned" the fire--one based on perceptions of which agency held legal responsibility for firefighting in that area.

An investigation showed that, based on land ownership, the responsibility for suppressing the fire lay with the BLM. Because the BLM contracts for firefighting with local firefighting organizations and the Oregon Department of Forestry, the responsibility was actually theirs. We quickly cleared up the structural issue and blame receded.

If we would have had time, firefighters could have suppressed the fire long before it exceeded initial-attack capability and became a crisis. That we were in crisis on a number of other fires was one of the main reasons that responsibility for Timbered Rock was not made clear quickly and the fire eventually "blew up."

Early in the fire season, a quick check of the maps and a few phone calls and the ODF and local firefighters would have "owned" the Timbered Rock Fire from the time of its ignition. In the intense "smoke" and distraction around firefighting in SW Oregon when Timbered Rock became a menace, responsibility was not particularly important to anyone. In the aftermath, however, as people moved to assign blame, responsibility became a primary focus.

Crisis Control along the Catastrophe Pathway

Pathway Stage	Distress	Scandal	Anarchy	Catastrophe
Issue	Structure	Structure	Structure	Structure
	Composition	Composition	Composition	Composition
	Function/Rela.	Function/Rela.	Function/Rela.	Function/Rela.
Full-blown Conflict	Structure	Structure	Structure	Structure
	Composition	Composition	Composition	Composition
	Function/Rela.	Function/Rela.	Function/Rela.	Function/Rela.
Crisis	Structure	Structure	Structure	Structure
	Composition	Composition	Composition	Composition
	Function/Rela.	Function/Rela.	Function/Rela.	Function/Rela.
Recovery	Structure	Structure	Structure	Structure
	Composition	Composition	Composition	Composition
	Function/Rela.	Function/Rela.	Function/Rela.	Function/Rela.

During the fires of 2002, much of the western U.S. felt the impacts of landscape-scale fires — big fires that are often hard to fight.

Crisis came to the Umpqua National Forest swiftly and in the night. A major lightening storm rolled through the area on July 11, and it left over 120 fires burning in the Umpqua Basin. The same series of storms ignited a complex of fires to the south that eventually became the Biscuit complex. *The Umpqua Fires of 2002* spells out the firefighting history of those times, and so I will not try to restate that history here.

Because this is a book about EDR, I will cover some of the aspects of the fast-moving crisis that was firefighting on the Umpqua in 2002. For my purposes, I will not detail the steps incident commanders and I took to control the fires themselves, but rather, look at the full-blown conflicts embedded in the crisis and at how we handled those conflicts.

There are things in my life that can cause me to panic, but fire and other emergencies are not among them. The worse the circumstances are, the calmer and more focused I become. So when the 2002 fires peppered the Umpqua Basin, I was concerned and focused, but not panicked. Our well-trained initial attack crews roared out to meet the fires, stopping those closest to towns and private property, and then moving back "up hill" to more remote sites. It was soon clear that we were approaching crisis because the assets under my immediate control were not even close to adequate to staff all the fires, let alone contain and suppress them.

Therefore, the first major crisis element was a dispute over the availability of people, equipment, and air assets. Large areas of the western U.S. were on fire too, including other large fires in Oregon, and assets were not available. In many cases, fires had been burning elsewhere for many weeks and exhausted crews wanted rest before they could mobilize to the Umpqua and other critical sites. Initially, acquiring air assets was also a dim hope for similar reasons.

The struggle for control of assets became a consistent theme for the 130 days of our record fire season. My staff could request assets, but those requests would often go unanswered. Frequent communications directly to those people doing the allocation proved to be only partially successful, whether the communications were sent by Incident Commands or Umpqua's fire staff.

It was only in late August, when I changed our position in the allocation system to benefit our fires, did we finally get needed resources headed our way. I changed that system by taking us out of an "area command," which had been put in place to control the allocation of assets and coordinate firefighting strategy, among other things. This departure was a change in a compositional factor and several functional and relationship factors; it allowed the Umpqua fires to receive assets separately from the Biscuit complex. We jumped from about fifth place for allocations nationally to second place.

Assets poured in. Some fires had been burning for over a month without staffing, but even so, we began to make significant progress.

Another compositional factor that I dealt with was the selection of tactics by the incident commanders. During the fire season, my employees and I had briefed in and briefed out 14 incident command teams from all over the U.S. As agency administrator, I had the responsibility for overseeing the firefighting and making sure it was successful. The operational aspects of the firefighting were primarily the responsibility of the incident commanders and their teams.

This is an effective system because it puts people with experience and expertise in direct day-to-day control of fighting the fires. However, the teams coming in from all over the nation had experience for many different ecoregions. Trained and equipped for fighting fire in other regions, some teams were more prepared, equipped, and adaptable than others.

For example, California teams were used to fighting brush fires, and their chain saws were often too short to handle our larger trees. They did fine if we gave them better tools and local fellers. Some teams from the Rockies were used to extensive burning out to clear fuels in advance of the main fire. Our fire conditions were such that burnouts had to be small, or the burn outs would become threats rather than controls. I had to intervene with incident teams to prevent large burnouts.

Some teams were used to working with collaborating agencies in joint commands, but others were not. To work within our complex Umpqua-basin system of firefighting agencies and inter-agency communications, teams had to receive support in establishing and maintaining effective communications and relationships with the local and state fire leaders. Some teams were better at community relations than others, but all of them had to receive assistance with their communications programs to some degree.

And so it went throughout the crisis, my staff and I handled a series of compositional and relationship issues and conflicts, **mending some, deflecting others, and taking control of still others to complete our mission to fight fire effectively and safely**.

Recovery along the Catastrophe Pathway

Pathway Stage	Distress	Scandal	Anarchy	Catastrophe
Issue	Structure	Structure	Structure	Structure
	Composition	Composition	Composition	Composition
	Function/Rela.	Function/Rela.	Function/Rela.	Function/Rela.
Full-blown Conflict	Structure	Structure	Structure	Structure
	Composition	Composition	Composition	Composition
	Function/Rela.	Function/Rela.	Function/Rela.	Function/Rela.
Crisis	Structure	Structure	Structure	Structure
	Composition	Composition	Composition	Composition
	Function/Rela.	Function/Rela.	Function/Rela.	Function/Rela.
Recovery	Structure	Structure	Structure	Structure
	Composition	Composition	Composition	Composition
	Function/Rela.	Function/Rela.	Function/Rela.	Function/Rela.

As was the case with the Timbered Rock Fire example, many issues went unaddressed during the crisis that pertained to the Umpqua fires and were topics for discussion during recovery. As with the Mio fire many years before, those recovery compositional and relationship issues associated with the 2002 fires took much longer to work through than the firefighting itself. In addition, as it is with other recovery situations, participants used blaming language as they presented and discussed many of the issues.

Most of these issues required a careful examination of the facts to move recovery along. For example, some people alleged federal firefighters were refusing assignments because of safety concerns even though the critics felt conditions allowed for safe firefighting. Different safety standards and threat perceptions among the agencies involved caused this compositional dispute to develop and linger. Agency staffs handled this dispute at the state and local level by reviewing firefighting safety standards and discussing wildfire conditions based on incident commend team records and anecdotes.

Another issue was the use of helicopter assets, particularly when a helicopter manager was not available. This was another compositional dispute handled at the state level.

Fire lines are strips of exposed mineral soil used to deny fuels to advancing ground fires. Sometimes firefighters will build a fire line by hand, and sometimes they use mechanical means, such as excavators and bulldozers (and rarely, they use explosives). The Forest Service actually designed the first bulldozer after World War I with this use in mind.

A local dispute concerned the extent and nature of the use of bulldozers to build fire lines. The dispute concerned our willingness to use bulldozers for the task. Critics held that Forest Service employees refused to use bulldozers at all, or when they did, they used them too sparingly, leaving fire lines too narrow.

One of the issues was compositional: were our bulldozer tactics consistent with good, safe firefighting tactics? We were able to answer that the uses were good and safe, and reflective of our concern for both containing the fires and protecting natural resources, such as rare plants, as well as cultural resources, such as Indian artifacts and burial sites. We also pointed out that bulldozer use depended, in part, on topography — steep country meant less use because it was unsafe.

Another of the issues was relational: how could private landowners trust us to manage our fires if we were not making maximum use of bulldozers? I replied that our record spoke for itself. For fires managed by the Umpqua National Forest, no private lands or property had been lost. In fact, with very few exceptions, no private property was even threatened.

Recovery could move forward. Blame diminished. Things got better. Planning and logistics for future fires became collaborative, slowly but surely, and local firefighting agencies began to look at joint command centers and more closely shared resources.

Chapter 6: Environmental Dispute Diagnosis

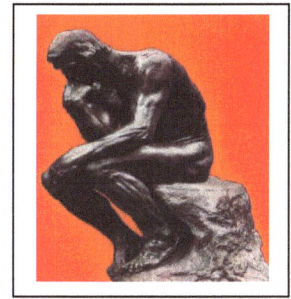

When asked how he made his remarkable statues, Francios-Auguste Rodin (1840-1917) said, *"I choose a block of marble and chop off whatever I don't need."* Like Rodin, EDR practitioners have to work to find the "hidden beauty" within an environmental dispute. A dispute diagnosis is very much about figuring out which of the 16 cells a dispute resides in, which of the factors within the cell(s) are most important to address, and artfully "carving off" those conditions or situations that won't contribute to a successful solution.

In the 2002 American Bar Association's EDR Anthology,[7] the authors provide some basic insights about a framework for analysis that includes a basic format to describe disputes:

- **participants** (disputants and other stakeholders)
- **actual and perceived conflicts** in needs and interests
- **facts or data conflicts** (actual and perceived differences over what is "true")
- **conflicts in fundamental values and priorities, and context** (administrative judicial, or legislative constraints, time and money constraints, power distribution).

The analytical components they list are certainly a portion of what we must consider in EDR work. However, their list is more a description of categories than it is a tool for diagnosis.

To be effective, we will need to go further, and so I offer a pathology-diagnosis-and treatment model in this book. Like medical professionals working to manage or cure disease, EDR practitioners want means and methods to diagnose the basis for disputes.

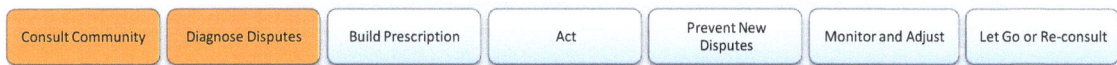

 Chapters 1-5 of this book describe the pathologies for treatment, Chapter 11 of the Theory and Principles book describes the conceptual prescriptive model, and this chapter covers community consultation and diagnosis. At the end of this chapter are some basic worksheets to assist the practitioner with diagnosis and documentation.   A more complete set of basic worksheets is located in Appendix B, pages 185 -190.

Defining and Consulting with the Community

I generally network extensively with the disputants and others in the community to get the names and contact information for likely dispute-resolution-community participants.

---

[7] *Environmental Dispute Resolution: An Anthology of Practical Solutions.* Eds. MacNaughton, Ann L. and Martin, Jay G. American Bar Association. 2002. pp.10-12.

The lists I create include the disputants themselves and their supporters or constituents, interested onlookers, directly and indirectly affected parties, and parties who will likely have to be involved in any management or resolution. They listed both as individuals and by their membership in communities of interest, place, tradition, or fate. My intention is to create complete but dynamic lists. As dispute intervention and management proceed, I revise the lists as my understanding grows.

If the intervention goes on long enough, list maintenance becomes a chore. I find that keeping up with the comings and goings of participants over several years can be relatively easy at the issue stage, but it is difficult and complex at the full-blown conflict, crisis, and recovery stages.

Along with the lists of participants, I try to capture the issues they care about and the values they hold about the issues and the dispute overall. I try to confirm those values over the course of the EDR effort by observing participants' statements and behavior and by asking questions at times when people seem to be experiencing strong motivation or emotion. People usually engage in the dispute and in EDR for relatively few reasons, so I find it critical to try to understand these behavioral motivators.

People generally want to fight or watch a fight; they generally do not want to do the hard work of environmental peacemaking. Thus, I have found that, as I make progress on the dispute, participant numbers drop, often significantly. Many times, disputants drop out, or they "step back" and let one disputant take the lead or even represent them. Constituents and onlookers lose interest, and general public interest declines. List management gets easier under these circumstances.

Stating the Subject and Outlining the Parameters of the Dispute

I begin the diagnosis by writing down the subject of the dispute in enough detail that disputants can affirm the subject's accuracy. Then I add descriptions of various parameters associated with the subject. Parameters include participants, stage, pathway, contributing factors, context and history, threat, and impediments. See the simple worksheet on page 73. This documentation is similar to taking a medical history.

EDR practitioners gather this information from a variety of sources, including the disputants, other participants, caring onlookers, and the media. Practitioners interpret the information and incorporate others' input, seeking both objective and subjective insights.

A thorough, but not necessarily exhaustive, knowledge of these parameters is required early in an EDR effort. This knowledge is necessary because the practitioner's credibility will rest, in part, on displaying that understanding to the disputants. In addition, the EDR practitioner will want to create positive momentum towards management or resolution actions as soon as possible and work cannot proceed without adequate background.

Diagnosis Step 1: Subject

Disputants will often have different descriptions of the topic, different views on whether distress, scandal, anarchy, or catastrophe forms the basis and means for describing the dispute. I find it convenient to record all the descriptions I hear when visiting the disputants and to use these descriptions to prepare a synthesis that reflects their words. Sometimes, when descriptions are highly specific or positional, I find it helpful to make the synthesis description more abstract, or to try to articulate what appears to be the personal or group values in conflict rather than the explicit dispute descriptions.

One reason for moving to higher-order abstraction and values articulation is to set the stage for values discussions and interest-based negotiations in the event they are desired later. In addition, later conflict resolution and crisis recovery efforts may only be successful and effective for the long term if EDR actions articulate, address, and reconcile underlying values conflicts in the search for transformation.

Diagnosis Step 2: Participants

Participants' descriptions include who the disputants are, the sub-groups within opposing groups, what constituencies the disputants depend upon, who the leaders are, and what values, strengths, and weaknesses the leaders hold. Looking beyond the disputants, descriptions include who now is or should be involved in management, resolution, control, and recovery so that measures taken can be effective – which means defining dispute communities and dispute-resolution communities.

Diagnosis Step 3: Stage

Stage	Distress	Scandal	Anarchy	Catastrophe
Issue	Structure	Structure	Structure	Structure
	Composition	Composition	Composition	Composition
	Function/Rela.	Function/Rela.	Function/Rela.	Function/Rela.
Full-blown Conflict	Structure	Structure	Structure	Structure
	Composition	Composition	Composition	Composition
	Function/Rela.	Function/Rela.	Function/Rela.	Function/Rela.
Crisis	Structure	Structure	Structure	Structure
	Composition	Composition	Composition	Composition
	Function/Rela.	Function/Rela.	Function/Rela.	Function/Rela.
Recovery	Structure	Structure	Structure	Structure
	Composition	Composition	Composition	Composition
	Function/Rela.	Function/Rela.	Function/Rela.	Function/Rela.

Oncologists classify cancers into four stages depending on severity. I also classify disputes into four stages: issue, full-blown conflict, crisis, and recovery. As it is with cancer, the four stages actually constitute a continuum from the easiest to cure to the most complex and difficult to treat, from the most innocuous and unthreatening to the most intrusive and potentially harmful or costly.

Descriptions should include distinctions among the positions, the object-, process-, rights-, and relationship-related values held by the disputants, and the material and social wants and needs expressed by the disputants.

Diagnosis Step 4: Pathway

Pathway	Distress	Scandal	Anarchy	Catastrophe
Issue	Structure	Structure	Structure	Structure
	Composition	Composition	Composition	Composition
	Function/Rela.	Function/Rela.	Function/Rela.	Function/Rela.
Full-blown Conflict	Structure	Structure	Structure	Structure
	Composition	Composition	Composition	Composition
	Function/Rela.	Function/Rela.	Function/Rela.	Function/Rela.
Crisis	Structure	Structure	Structure	Structure
	Composition	Composition	Composition	Composition
	Function/Rela.	Function/Rela.	Function/Rela.	Function/Rela.
Recovery	Structure	Structure	Structure	Structure
	Composition	Composition	Composition	Composition
	Function/Rela.	Function/Rela.	Function/Rela.	Function/Rela.

I assess the pathway (or pathways) by evaluating the nature and content of the dispute communications and structural factors, like ecological or legal conditions.

Diagnosis Step 5: Contributing Factors

Pathway / Stage	Distress	Scandal	Anarchy	Catastrophe
Issue	Structure	Structure	Structure	Structure
	Composition	Composition	Composition	Composition
	Function/Rela.	Function/Rela.	Function/Rela.	Function/Rela.
Full-blown Conflict	Structure	Structure	Structure	Structure
	Composition	Composition	Composition	Composition
	Function/Rela.	Function/Rela.	Function/Rela.	Function/Rela.
Crisis	Structure	Structure	Structure	Structure
	Composition	Composition	Composition	Composition
	Function/Rela.	Function/Rela.	Function/Rela.	Function/Rela.
Recovery	Structure	Structure	Structure	Structure
	Composition	Composition	Composition	Composition
	Function/Rela.	Function/Rela.	Function/Rela.	Function/Rela.

Practitioners should describe the structure, composition, and functions or relationships contributing to the dispute, including relationships among the disputants and between the disputants and government entities and nongovernmental organizations. If appropriate, practitioners can add ecological functions and scale. Write-ups should also capture differing perceptions among disputants and other participants as to why the dispute exists, focusing on relations among disputants and larger communities.

I usually write up the principal contributing factors based on communications with the disputants and other participants. Because the values conflicts can be so great, and values may be the only expressions, sometimes I have to propose and confirm what the contributing factors seem to be and how they apply to the dispute. I then confirm and clarify that set of assumptions with the participants.

Diagnosis Step 6: Context and History

History refers to the background against which the dispute takes place, and it can include the history of the area and of the dispute up to the present, past definitions of the subject, participants, stages, and contributing factors. I usually do a short write-up of the history to help form a benchmark for dispute-resolution progress.

Practitioners should describe the context, including intensity and duration, connections to other disputes or processes (such as political proposals), and past communications, including message and medium. Practitioners may want to map the dispute area and the values in conflict if pertinent — maps can display both past and present information.

I usually create a simple diagram of the disputes and their connections. Sometimes, higher-order disputes, such as those at the national policy level, will influence the timing and outcome of more local disputes. A vigorous local effort can also play a major role in informing and affecting higher-order disputes, too. Maps showing dispute connections at different scales can be useful.

In addition, because communications plays a key role in EDR work, an understanding of past messages and media use is important. I sometimes convey the information in the history. Other times, when the background is replete with poor communications and impaired media, I will comment on past communications separately.

Diagnosis Step 7: Threat

A threat assessment is composed of evaluations of risk, vulnerability, and consequences. EDR practitioners can compute risk statistically or ask participants to express it subjectively, perhaps as an estimate. Vulnerability refers to what qualities of life are at risk. Items that might be vulnerable include structural factors such as natural resources or law, compositional factors such as business activities or working agreements, or relationship factors such as partnerships, collaborations, or friendships. Consequences can include direct and indirect impacts, such as ecological declines or improvements, human losses, or gains in quality of life.

An important benchmark for threat assessments and applications is to describe likely scenarios for what will happen if the dispute goes unaddressed. The context of the dispute is a good place to look for elements in which to ground the no-action description and analogies to other, similar disputes too. The description should state clearly that analogies and comparisons are imperfect. Anecdotes, oral histories, and story telling can enhance this sort of benchmark narrative.

Diagnosis Step 8: Impediments

As a part of the worksheets, EDR practitioners may also want to identify and document some common impediments to EDR effectiveness that appear to be present, similar to how a doctor might note attitudes or behaviors exhibited by a patient that could prevent effective treatment. In her book, Laurie Coltri describes fourteen impediments[8]:

1. Motivation to seek **vengeance**
2. Meta-disputes (disputes about **how disputes are handled**)
3. **Mistrust**
4. Vastly different **perceptions of reality**
5. **Over-commitment and entrapment** (a disputant over-commits and cannot reverse their position later)
6. Lack of **ripeness** (disputants do not agree on the dispute's urgency)
7. **Jackpot Syndrome** (one disputant looks for a big, unrealistic payoff)
8. **Loss aversion** (mainly object- or power-related loss)
9. **Linkages** (to other disputes, opportunities, or among disputants and partners)
10. **Conflicts of interest** (team members and powerful people)
11. **Excluded stakeholders** (caring onlookers, other participants, powerful people)
12. **Disempowered** disputant
13. **Unpleasant** disputant
14. **Competitive culture or subculture**

To Coltri's list, I add seven more impediments that apply to environmental disputes:

15. Preoccupation with **risk and uncertainty** (like #8 but process- or rights-related)
16. Over-interpretation or misinterpretation of the **meaning and effect of science** findings and knowledge
17. **Professional arrogance or self-righteous thinking and behavior**
18. **Single-resource or single-issue focus**
19. **Scapegoating, blaming, and diminishment**
20. **Exiting** (leaving the dispute-resolution community) physically, mentally, and/or emotionally
21. Failure to accept the **reality of structure, composition, function or relationship, and ecological-scale factors**

---

[8]*Conflict Diagnosis and Alternative Dispute Resolution.* Coltri, Laurie S. Pearson Education, Inc. Upper Saddle River, NJ. 2004. pp.192-214.

In the next chapter, I will discuss techniques used for issues abatement, conflict resolution, or crisis control and recovery; and in the following chapters, I will offer a prescriptive approach that will help EDR practitioners and leaders to select and apply effective techniques to disputes and then monitor for results.

Reviewing the list of 21 impediments, practitioners should document their perceptions of the impediments to successful EDR for each group or participant. This list will be useful for all aspects of EDR, including orientation, training, and education efforts, designing individual and group communications means and messages, and structuring meetings and group activities.

Diagnosis Step 9: People with the Power to Ensure EDR Success

Sometimes experts perform a "power analysis" to determine who holds what power with respect to the dispute. In this context, they describe power relationships among disputants, whether they are symmetric or asymmetric, and the means for exerting these powers.

Whether a power analysis is prepared or not, an important element of the diagnosis is the identification of those people with the effective power to support the EDR effort and whose consent will be needed for the EDR effort to be successful. These individuals should be identified, contacted, and engaged early and often throughout the effort. Agreements should be revisited at regular intervals. Scale is important in EDR and also for defining power-cooperators. EDR leaders and practitioners should be looking for power-contacts at least one scale higher and one scale lower than the dispute scale.

Diagnosis Step 10: Creating the Report

On the next page is a simple form to document and report your diagnosis. The report is a dynamic document, the first write-up useful as a benchmark for future reference as your knowledge and understanding of the dispute grows. Therefore, store the various versions of the report, dating them for future reference.

The report is replete with assumptions and interpretations. Thus, to assure that the descriptions are valid, consultation and confirmation with disputants and key onlookers is essential.

If the dispute is in the issue stage, validation can be as simple as handing the report to disputants and, after discussion, asking them if it is accurate. Sometimes, EDR practitioners can build the report with the open, direct involvement of the disputants and interested onlookers, using an interactive, "fishbowl" approach.

Subject

1.	What is (are) the topic(s) of this dispute?

Parameters

2.	Who are the participants and what are their values concerning this dispute?	<ul><li>Disputants</li><li>Caring onlookers</li><li>Dispute community</li><li>Dispute-resolution community</li></ul>
3.	What stage is the dispute in and why?	<ul><li>Issue</li><li>Full-blown conflict</li><li>Crisis</li><li>Recovery</li></ul>
4.	What pathway(s) is (are) the dispute traveling and why?	<ul><li>Distress</li><li>Scandal</li><li>Anarchy</li><li>Catastrophe</li></ul>
5.	What are the contributing factors?	<ul><li>Structural</li><li>Compositional</li><li>Functional/Relationship</li></ul>
6.	What is the context and history of the dispute?	<ul><li>Context</li><li>History</li><li>Connections to other disputes</li><li>Past communications</li><li>Dispute scale (attach maps, if needed)</li></ul>
7.	What are the threats inherent in this dispute?	<ul><li>Risks</li><li>Vulnerabilities</li><li>Consequences</li><li>No-action and no-resolution consequences</li></ul>
8.	What are the impediments to success held by the disputants and essential participants?	<ul><li>Impediments by participant</li></ul>
9.	Who are the powerful people who must support or consent to the EDR effort for it to be successful?	<ul><li>At your dispute's scale</li><li>At higher scale(s)</li><li>At lower scales(s)</li></ul>

If the dispute is more complex and intense, validation may occur through a structured, one-on-one conversation with the separate disputants, using the report questions and answers as a reference rather than as a document text for review. This is simply to reduce the potential for inciting the disputants, for increasing their tendency to take entrenched positions, and their alienation from one another. A summary report is then prepared with the many viewpoints noted.

The report is also an important first step in creating a prescription based on applicable techniques, but this set of actions cannot begin until initial validation of the report is complete.

Done well, report validation is a very useful step that sets the stage for defining which combination of stage and pathway to address. Done poorly, EDR practitioners themselves may be viewed as disputants rather than helpers, positional rather than neutral.

Chapter 7: Setting Strategy, Goals, and Objectives for EDR

Yogi Berra said, *"You got to be careful if you don't know where you're going, because you might not get there."* It is good to have a target in mind when beginning EDR work, particularly for groups, even if the target changes over time. Otherwise, it is hard to describe or experience success, to evaluate progress, or to reflect on how much progress is being made.

This chapter builds on the previous chapter about EDR diagnosis. In this chapter we begin making some decisions about what direction to go and fixes to try. In addition, if important decisions by disputants and other participants are a likely outcome of the dispute-resolution effort, EDR goals and objectives can reflect the decision-making efforts and contribute to them. This is true whether practitioners are using a problem solving or a visionary-opportunistic decision-making model.

Putting EDR Program Direction Together

Once EDR leaders select a strategy, the first step in prescribing EDR actions is to set a tentative direction for the actions to take. I always try to set a realistic goal for the practitioner and the disputants as well as for other participants. For example, as I worked

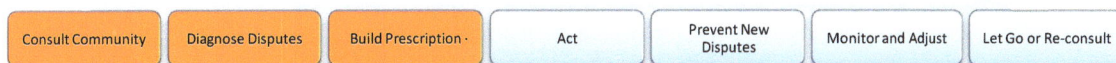

| Consult Community | Diagnose Disputes | Build Prescription · | Act | Prevent New Disputes | Monitor and Adjust | Let Go or Re-consult |

with the timber industry and the environmental groups who opposed one another in the Umpqua Valley, I set a stretch goal: the participants being able to sit in the same room or visit a field site and have a civil conversation. I repeated this goal several times over the course of a year or so, and they were, in fact, eventually able to speak civilly on all topics.

It is fine if the goal seems to be a stretch for the current situation. Setting a stretch goal with the involvement of the disputants begins the re-imaging of the dispute. Although everyone involved may be skeptical of the possibility of attaining the goal, the effort is well worth the time spent.

Sometimes, practitioners may find that the dispute is in or near crisis and related events are moving too fast for goal setting. Practitioners should still "toss one out" and to disputants if for no other reason than to create a concept to revisit later during recovery.

The importance of the goal in the psychological sense is that, by working on and at least tentatively committing to achieving the goal, the disputants are taking the first step in lowering resistance and reducing tensions. Practitioners should treat this step with respect and view it as the first movement towards trust development and resolution.

Once the goal is fairly well established (and that might be only an initial hour's work), objectives should be set that, if each is fully accomplished, would add up to attaining the goal or goals. So, because fully met objectives define goal-attainment, and thereby success, they should be as measurable as possible in order to help EDR practitioners and disputants define the milestones of the journey and to reach the destination.

If they can be set, physically or numerically measurable objectives are great. However, if what we are trying to achieve is subjective or "normative," such as someone's mood state or sense of trust for their disputants' values or behaviors, then we will ask disputants and other participants to help describe these components as accurately as possible. We will then check in with the same people later to see if those conditions were attained.

This testing of hard-to-measure conditions is one place where the observations and opinions of caring onlookers and other participants can be valuable for practitioners and disputants alike. People working on EDR and intensely involved in the effort cannot easily maintain objectivity about progress. People observing that effort and caring about resolution often are impartial and actually watching to see if change is occurring.

I knew I had achieved an important objective in my work with the timber and environmental representatives when each side was able to state the key values held by the other concerning mature forest management on the Umpqua National Forest clearly and publicly. I believe it was a profound moment for many of the folks participating because, for the first time perhaps ever, they heard their disputants say that they had heard them and understood the values about which they cared. After that, they were not able to claim misunderstanding of one another's values, and within a year, we had achieved a breakthrough in commitment by both sides to restorative forestry in mature forests.

In 2006, the controversial Umpqua National Forest exceeded its timber target by 32% with no litigation. The 2007 program went forward with no appeals or litigation, exceeding the annual target by at least 25%. Broad-based public support is worth attaining.

Goal Setting

As a public-agency representative, I felt Constitutionally bound to seek dispute resolution leading to environmental peace and justice for Americans, and so, in one sense, that made goal setting fairly easy for me. I could state the goal as "disputants x and y find environmental peace and justice and resolve their dispute over z and are not concerned about this dispute arising again."

For other situations, and for practitioners who entertain less-lofty goals, the goal might speak more directly to resolving the dispute. In this context, an initial goal statement might be "disputants x and y have resolved their dispute over z and are not concerned about this dispute arising again."

Objectives Setting

In Chapter 6, I discussed dispute diagnosis. Readers learned how to evaluate dispute stages and how to create a basic understanding of the dispute structure, composition, and relationship factors. Ideas presented in the Theory and Principles book demonstrated how all disputes arise from conflicting value-preference scales that lead to people's behavior and actions. Psychological mechanisms such as fright responses, transference, projection, resistance, and blame attribution also influence behavior.

As objectives are set to attain the goal, the objectives can reflect all of these factors and elements. To make the process go smoothly, I try to build objectives based on the structural, compositional, and relationship factors. I tend to sort these from the more difficult factors in order to better recognize and operationalize psychological and social elements into the three factor categories.

Structure: the physical, biological, legal, political, economic, and ecological aspects of the dispute, characterized geographically when possible.

Composition: the people, their values, interpretations of structural elements, and the means of public and private communications and interactions that exist within the structure.

Functions or Relationships: human-to-human and human-to-nature relationships, how one uses, works with, or changes another, and the content of communications as symbolic of and conducive to human relationships and desired outcomes. Functional and relationship elements include human uses of nature (sometimes called "ecological services"), the flow of solar and other energy, and the effects of human stewardship of ecosystems.

Four chapters following the next chapter on techniques explore objectives setting at each dispute stage, with objectives-setting presented as part of an integrated EDR program, tailored to the specifics of each dispute. The discussion in those four chapters builds on the general objectives-framework presentation made here.

Chapter 8: Dispute-Resolution Techniques

Techniques in General

Someone once said, *"To a hammer, every job is a nail."* A hammer is not a saw. A hammer will not cut a board, but instead, may smash it. A saw will not drive a nail except by damaging the saw. Picking techniques suitable for use on the dispute at hand will be critical for your EDR success. Technique/tool confusion in EDR is common, and practitioners are obliged to make effective technique choices before proceeding with an EDR effort. Moreover, EDR technique has to be sensitive to objectives set for the EDR effort and to the social and cultural capabilities of the participants.

Consult Community	Diagnose Disputes	Build Prescription	Act	Prevent New Disputes	Monitor and Adjust	Let Go or Re-consult

This chapter lists techniques for addressing disputes, describing the techniques and offering some insights into use. Later chapters will demonstrate how to apply techniques to disputes depending on stage and on structural, compositional, and functional or relationship factors.

Some techniques have broad application and some apply narrowly. For example, some techniques only have value for triggering a crisis, a very delicate action that must only be undertaken thoughtfully and carefully. Other techniques, such as third-party neutral mediation, can apply to almost every dispute stage with varying emphasis and varying likelihood of success.

German master architect Ludwig Mies van der Rohe (1886-1969) was one of modern architecture's leaders. He created many famous structures of glass and steel, austere and beautiful. We also remember him for these statements: *"less is more"* and *"God is in the details."* He conveyed those ideas in his work, and both concepts apply equally well to EDR. Consistent his thoughts, EDR technique numbers must be held to the minimum required to resolve the disputes at hand. And, once chosen, techniques must be implemented in sufficient detail to achieve EDR objectives.

Just as there are many choices in minimalist, utilitarian architecture, we have almost too many EDR techniques to count. Depending on the intended goals and objectives for the EDR effort, many techniques could get the job done. One of the great advantages of having so many choices is that, if one technique does not pan out, EDR practitioners and participants can switch to other techniques. This chapter presents many techniques, but I offer these simply as a "sampler," and readers are encouraged to look long and widely for other useful EDR tools and invent some of their own.

Practitioners and caring onlookers should consider adopting Thomas Alva Edison's (1847-1931) idea: *"I have not failed. I've just found*

10,000 ways that won't work." Edison was famous for his dogged pursuit of results, and EDR workers must be dogged in their pursuit of resolution as well.

Legal Context for Using Techniques

Most EDR work is done "in the shadow of the law," which refers to the legal and regulatory aspects of disputes, the structural factors associated with almost every environmental dispute. These factors are continuously present in any society like ours that governs itself by the "rule of law" rather than depending on personalities or the force of arms for order. Remembering that we are conducting EDR in the shadow of the law also emphasizes the importance of legislative bodies and the courts in helping with structural and compositional changes if practitioners and participants want to implement such changes as part of an EDR.

Recognizing the Value of both "Strong" and "Weak" Components in Dispute Resolution

Regardless of the methods chosen, practitioners can guide disputants and participants in formalizing a series of decisions about events or outcomes. Practitioners and participants usually document decisions explicitly, and these decisions constitute some of the "strong" components of the dispute resolution. Many times, the strong components are structural in nature: changes in geographic boundary or law, permanent changes in resource ownership, or a new managing agency, for example. Strong components are valuable and necessary, but alone they may not be sufficient for long-term dispute resolution.

A whole series of minor changes in perceptions, attitudes, communication patterns and content, and relationships constitute "weak" components. Added to strong components, weak components may be exactly what practitioners and participants require to create transformations and long-term resolution.

Physicists consider gravity a "weak force," and yet gravity makes life possible on Earth. Similarly, depending on the dispute, the weak components, in sum, may bring about a more significant impact than the strong components in settling a dispute or handling recovery. Too much emphasis on strong component changes, such a change in federal law, can leave the underlying dispute in place and aggravate disputants with extended time delays. At the same time, too much emphasis on the weak components may mean that disputants will not have any clear milestones or conclusions to reference.

Many times, weak components go undocumented, and in fact, it is a judgment call about

how explicit documentation should be. My experience is that more documentation should occur than often does because future understanding of weak agreements and practices will be highly subjective unless there are at least reference notes. Although some of these weak components might be structural in nature (e.g., a 2-year no-litigation consent agreement), in most cases, the weak elements are compositional or functional/relationship.

Third Party Neutrals and Interveners

I find many people emphasizing neutral third-party intervention as the means to manage and resolve environmental disputes. This "family" of techniques can be thought of as a spectrum that runs from informal to formal and it can involve expertise ranging from caring, committed amateurs to highly trained professionals.

The most informal and least-trained might be an **uninvolved, respected local person** who agrees to sit down with disputants and attempt to achieve resolution. Some cultures acknowledge specific people for this role and may even nurture their development as they mature. For example, **Navajo "peace chiefs"**[9] are civil leaders who embody cultural values; their communities also know them to be moral and ethical people who can guide others and plan for community survival and continuity.

Sometimes, **fact-finding boards, committees, or blue-ribbon panels** assist EDR efforts. Powerful people usually appoint the groups because of their credibility and expertise, and sometimes because of their political connections and influence. These groups can be invaluable in EDR efforts by providing impartial and expert insight into any dispute factor, and by offering potential solutions. If they have political influence, their involvement may enhance the social and political feasibility of EDR settlements and agreements. Disputants may be tempted to try to control the group's mandate, charter, or rules of engagement, and this may be only a distraction, or worse (if one disputant prevails) undermine the group's EDR effectiveness.

If the groups convene for a limited period, EDR participants may find their value and effectiveness to be transitory. If groups issue reports, the positive effects can last longer, but sometimes, what goes unstated in the report is as valuable as the report itself. If groups present only consensus information, they will omit the valuable insights and creative ideas offered by dissenters. If EDR practitioners act quickly before memories fade, they can contact members or staff supporting the groups to gain those dissenting insights.

Sometimes, authorities or the courts appoint a **sanctioning board or committee** that can authorize, limit, or otherwise regulate actions. Such groups can provide long-term oversight and direction to an EDR implementation effort, particularly ones managed adaptively.

Conciliation or reconciliation boards[10] **or committees** are a variation on the concepts behind fact-finding, blue ribbon, and sanctioning groups. These groups focus on

---

[9] "The Dynamics of Navajo Peacemaking". James W. Zion. Northern Arizona University. *Journal of Contemporary Criminal Justice,* Vol. 14 No. 1, February 1998 58-74. Sage Publications, Inc.

[10] Truth and Reconciliation Committee (TRC) By Alistair Boddy-Evans, About.com

rebuilding compositional, functional, and relationship elements between disputants, usually after a crisis. Powerful people usually appoint the members because of their public credibility and expertise, their reputations as peacemakers, and sometimes because of their cultural or religious connections and influence. The members of these groups must perform, and be recognized as, conciliation and reconciliation process advocates and stewards. If people begin to perceive them as biased or as favoring one disputant over another, they may lose their effectiveness. The **Federal Mediation and Conciliation Service** (www.fmcs.gov) is an agency that provides this service in labor-management disputes.

The authors of *Contemporary Conflict Resolution* relate differing views of reconciliation efforts, but the fundamental need is for public acknowledgement of past hurts, which allows disputants, victim and oppressor alike, to move on from rage and hatred to the acceptance of loss, of the status quo, and each other.[11]

Another source of EDR support may come from voluntary, often self-appointing and self-managing "**peace brigades**"[12] or "**peace factions.**" These are groups of citizens, often caring onlookers, who form a group to support the EDR effort specifically. Their focus is on mobilizing social and political support for peace and justice. They can be invaluable in gaining attention for EDR efforts and mobilizing concerned citizens and groups. They may also be beneficial in gaining favorable attention for the EDR effort. They can help practitioners accomplish far more than the practitioners could accomplish on their own. If their focus changes from support for the EDR goal and processes to support for one disputant over another, or for specific settlement options, however, they may lose their credibility and effectiveness.

Traditional Christian communities established **safe havens, safe harbors,** or **sanctuaries** within churches where secular authority could not make arrests or harm fugitives. As long as the fugitives remained within the sanctuary (the actual name today of the altar area of many churches) they were safe. In EDR, a **safe haven meeting** might include bringing a dispute community to a neutral site after establishing firm agreements about **rules of engagemen**t--strict rules designed to keep all parties feeling safe.

The use of an expert **mediator**[13] is more formal than work done by a respected local person or blue-ribbon group. Most mediators have specialized training, and many are attorneys educated to conduct mediation to achieve agreements for eventual consideration by the courts. EDR efforts may also ask **"peer" mediators** to participate because of their associations with disputants, professional credibility, and community-wide respect. Peer mediators are usually trained non-professionals with credibility in specific communities of interest, place, tradition, or fate.

---

[11] *Contemporary Conflict Resolution: The prevention, management, and transformation of deadly conflicts, Second Edition.* Ramsbotham, Oliver, Woodhouse, Tom, and Miall, Hugh. Polity Press, Malden, MA. 2005. p.243.

[12] www.peacebrigades.org

[13] *Mediation in a Nutshell.* Kovach, Kimberlee K. West Group, St. Paul, MN. 2003. and *Mediate, Don't Litigate: Strategies for Successful Mediation.* Lovenheim, Peter and Guerin, Lisa. Nolo, Berkeley, CA. 2004.

Sometimes communities or agencies hire mediators to assist with improving communications and defining options. Mediators may also serve to convene meetings and facilitate values discussions, bringing disputants together to seek resolution.

Mediators usually strive to be fully inclusive and have their work fully open to scrutiny. For example, they usually do not meet with one disputant separate from the other unless the other disputant agrees, and they use the "**one text**[14]" or "**common text**" method of developing agreements. "One text" simply means that disputants are working on the same text or identical copies of the text at any given time. Disputants selecting a non-attorney mediator may later employ one to complete a formal agreement if they want a written resolution agreement adequate for court approval.

Negotiators have different roles from mediators because the nature of the negotiations process is often more formal and structured. Negotiators assist or represent disputants in a negotiation. Sometimes, disputants set the negotiation rules or a contract, law, or the courts may impose them. Professional negotiators often work to set an agenda, develop a schedule, assist with assembling expert analysis and information, and participate in face-to-face talks. They also assist with the use of negotiation tactics, some of which may facilitate EDR by building trust and collaboration while other tactics may be coercive or punitive, resulting in low trust and issue recycling.

If disputants choose to use an **arbitrator**, a formal arbitration agreement often spells out the arbitrator's role. Disputants usually select the arbitrator from a list of certified arbitrators in their locale.

An arbitrator may act much like a mediator at times. However, an arbitrator is usually an attorney, perhaps a retired judge, who brings legal interpretations and arguments into the inter-disputant dialogs. The arbitrator may gather evidence independently, hold hearings, and create a written record of those hearings, perhaps with a court recorder. Sometimes, legal counsel represents disputants in working through disputes with an arbitrator.

Disputants choosing "**binding arbitration**" essentially cede outcome control to the arbitrator or arbitration panel. The term "binding" means that the disputants' arbitration agreement states that the arbitrators' decision will control the outcome. Usually binding arbitration resembles a court hearing at some point, although one difference is that, unlike judges, arbitrators sometimes investigate, assemble, and review information on their own, ask for negotiation on some points, and conduct informal, off-the-record resolution discussions with disputants. A single arbitrator or an arbitration panel may make arbitration decisions.

---

[14] "Three Models for Implementing Change in 21st Century Schools." Tyler-Wood, C. Mark Smith, and Charles Barker. *Journal of the North American Association of Educational Negotiators and The Negotiator Magazine.* January 2008

EDR practitioners may also recommend the use of a **referee or umpire** to assist disputants who are working on an agreement or trying to establish norms in their relationship. The referee or umpire makes sure that disputants follow mutually agreed-to rules of engagement. Umpires and referees should have authority to make quick calls on complaints about rules infringement. As in sports, referees and umpires facilitate the "action" and assure that disputants are "safe" within the context of the EDR effort. Courts or contract requirements sometimes call for umpires and referees.

From time to time, a court, arbitration panel, agency, community, or collaborative group may appoint a **"permanent" umpire, facilitator, mediator, or arbitrator** to assist with long-term implementation and maintenance of agreements. The person also likely serves to present dispute recycling by assisting with issue abatement long-term. For the individual to be effective, they must have clear authority and direction for their work, usually spelled out in the EDR settlement agreement and any personal-services contract.

Some governments and businesses may offer an **ombudsman**[15] **or ombuds-board** to assist with EDR. Because of the nature of their work, many ombudsmen are attorneys and understand legal requirements. They offer great insight for how things work under

current laws and regulations, but they rarely have decision-making authority.

The original concept of ombudsman was a person who anonymously represented the interests of common citizens to sovereign authority, a voice for the people that bypassed bureaucracies and communication barriers. The ombudsman concept emphasized early-intervention in disputes and issues-abatement.

Today's American ombudsmen may not operate within the original concept, and EDR practitioners should understand the legal, political, and time-availability limits on an ombudsman before trying to use their expertise.

EDR practitioners may have to employ other categories of third-party interveners from time to time to add content and insight into existing conditions, provide advice about change, or help people in distress. These include **health-care professionals** such as **mental health and stress counselors**, and other specialists such as **decision scientists, historians, sociologists, economists, ethicists, ethnologists, communication specialists, and community- and economic-development experts**.

Many environmental disputes involve disagreements over the interpretation and application of science findings and expert knowledge. Both science and expert knowledge are constantly changing, moving targets. Therefore, EDR practitioners should consider using **science advisors and reviewers, or perhaps sciences panels and committees, as well as peer-review methods** to assure that the science and knowledge

---

[15] www.ombudsman.gov

that participants bring to the EDR table is state-of-the-art. These methods vary somewhat from one science or professional discipline to another, but specific protocols are usually easy to obtain from scientific or professional societies and oversight groups.

A special form of third-party intervener is the "**maven,**" a term that comes from Yiddish culture and public relations tradecraft. A maven is a go-to person, a trusted advisor to influential or powerful people, or to an entire network of people and institutions. Some EDR and public relations experts emphasize discovering who these mavens are and opening clear communications with them early in an EDR effort in order to influence the understanding and behavior of decision makers and entire communities.

Although EDR practitioners hire third-party interveners for their expertise and the content or service they provide, third-parties may also assist with activities to develop trust and collaboration. For example, a sociologist may also be an expert facilitator, or an archeologist might have a very close relationship with an Indian tribe that allows for trusting communications during a dispute.

Chapter 1 of the Theory and Principles book displays a diagram of cost versus satisfaction, showing that satisfaction often declines as dollar, time, and loss-of-relationship costs increase. In addition, as costs go up and satisfaction goes down, the nature of the dispute intervention by third parties changes from informal to formal. Moreover, control over outcomes tends to decline as the intervention formalizes because, if disputants choose binding arbitration or litigation as the third-party-intervention technique, the arbitrators or the judge make the outcome decision unless the disputants choose to settle before receiving a decision.

Therefore, the decision to move from informal ("friendly") intervention to mediation, from mediation to negotiation, from negotiation to arbitration, from arbitration to binding arbitration, or from binding arbitration to litigation is a major decision. The costs go up as satisfaction and outcome-control may decline.

A Few Caveats about Third-Party Interveners

I caution people about the use of third-party neutral interveners. These capable professionals are an excellent choice in many disputes, a viable means to an end. However, like all "tools in a tool chest," their use depends on the desired dispute-resolution outcome. They may be the wrong tool for the circumstances, and their use, or their use at the wrong time, can actually make disputes worse.

It is important to understand which powers and authorities those who are party to a dispute actually have; in the same vein, it is important to understand the authority for using third parties, if any exists.

If the legal structure behind the dispute does not allow or, even better, require their use, third-party interveners can waste time and money. If mediation is voluntary, one disputant may agree to mediation as a delaying tactic while they increase support for their position and work to frustrate their disputants politically or through later litigation. Public agency people may not have the latitude to use third parties or accept the outcome of their work, even if disputants voluntarily use them. If law or contract requires mediation, or disputants sincerely commit to mediation, the potential for effective dispute-resolution goes up dramatically.

Sometimes, mediation or other third-party intervention sets a baseline for further EDR work. If participants and onlookers understand that third-party work will only take EDR work so far, and that further development is required to reach a settlement, then the third-party work can be effective. Failing that understanding, the perception of underachievement may cause the third-party work to fail or be impaired.

Compositional issues about the use of third parties may also impair performance. Some individuals and cultures support or tolerate third-party intervention, and others do not. And, in many cases **who** the interveners are and **what they symbolize** to disputants become critical factors to consider — as critical as technical competence. **Trust and credibility** are critical factors; if they do not exist initially or do not develop quickly, the third-party effort will likely go nowhere.

Roger Sidaway[16] states that mediation is most likely to be successful if:
- There is a history of cooperation and actions in good faith
- The numbers of participants and level of anger is low
- The working relationship is valuable to everyone
- Disputants are willing to accept help
- There is pressure from outside to settle
- An impasse has been reached
- Agreement is within the groups' power
- Representatives are trusted and have some flexibility
- Relevant information is available

Sidaway further states that mediation is less likely to be successful if:
- The disputants hold fundamentally contradictory values
- Many people are involved and key people are not available
- A larger issue (perhaps national scale) is at stake in a local dispute
- Representatives and authorities are lacking
- Long-term consequences of settlement and action are not clear

EDR practitioners will find Sidaway's insights valuable in deciding whether to employ mediation.

In addition to Sidaway's ideas, practitioners should understand that public agencies and private corporations often have administrative means to redress grievances that prevent or limit mediation. For example, the USDI Bureau of Land Management uses an

---

[16] *Resolving Environmental Disputes: From Conflict to Consensus.* Sidaway, Roger. Sterling, VA. 2005. p.84

administrative "protest" process and later-stage proceedings before the Interior Board of Land Appeals, an administrative law court for redress of grievances short of full-blown litigation. Private corporations may have contractual agreements with their clients that require binding arbitration in lieu of litigation. The work of third-party interveners may enhance these dispute-resolution processes, but disputants and interveners must give credence to existing processes in any dispute affecting the agencies or corporations.

Meeting Styles

A third-party neutral intervener, any party to a dispute, or a caring onlooker may decide to call a meeting to work on an environmental dispute. Many meeting choices are available, depending on the desired outcome. One style definitely does not suit every dispute, and the meeting design may vary by the dispute's stage or structure.

These days, I divide meetings into two broad categories: facilitated and leader-directed. I rarely encounter a third category, which consists of agenda-less or self-directed meetings. This category of meeting is usually a part of teambuilding or brainstorming exercises. As mentioned in Chapter 10 of the Theory and Principles book, where I discuss autocratic versus inclusive management styles, different management styles often use different communications styles. Likewise, they also often use different meeting styles.

Autocratic leaders frequently select leader-directed meetings, wherein they control all meeting elements, including the outcomes. In its extreme form, autocratic managers ask information of meeting participants, direct the discussion, and announce the decisions with little participant engagement.

Leader-directed meetings can deliver one-direction information and decisions efficiently. If buy-in by others is important for success, however, leader-directed meetings can be ineffective.

Inclusive managers and leaders frequently use facilitated meetings not only to elicit expert information from groups but also to gain people's commitment and participation in making and implementing decisions. In its extreme form, inclusive leaders and managers never make decisions themselves, but instead, guide others to serve as decision-makers.

In How to Make Meetings Work: the New Interaction Method,[17] the authors describe the pattern of facilitated meetings to include a leader, a recorder, a facilitator, and one or more subject-matter experts. The leader makes sure the meeting stays focused on a desired outcome. The recorder keeps an accurate record for the benefit of the whole group. The facilitator makes sure the group stays on task and schedule. The subject-

---

[17] How to Make Meetings Work: the New Interaction Method. Doyle, Michael and Strauss, Larry. Penguin Putnam Books. New York, NY. 1982.

matter experts provide the reliable and credible information that the group requires to make effective decisions or to gain information about key issues and conditions.

Many variants on this basic facilitation model exist. Regardless of staffing, for facilitation to work, an EDR practitioner must understand and respect the four elements of leader, facilitator, recorder, and expert. Sometimes groups sophisticated in the method self-facilitate, sharing and trading off the key roles in a smooth and seamless fashion.

Facilitated meetings can be inefficient as regards time and topics unless the leader, facilitator, and experts respect and follow the ground rules established for the facilitation process. When done well, facilitated meetings deliver information and decisions more efficiently and effectively than directed meetings. When done poorly, facilitated meetings can devolve into debates and disagreements, accomplishing nothing.

Meeting Types

A meeting requires at least two people and a place. Sometimes the place is "virtual" (connected technologically, but participants are not necessarily in the same place and perhaps not participating at the same time), and sometimes it involves having the participants in the same room.

Regardless of whether meetings are virtual or in-person, meetings range along a continuum from highly structured to highly flexible. For example, a **formal business meeting** is likely to be highly structured and have a published agenda, featured speakers, and a carefully adhered to schedule. A **charette or brainstorming meeting** can be highly flexible, with loosely defined goals or expectations and a simple process responsive to participants' values about meetings and to changing information.

Some meetings are specifically **agenda-free** to allow participants to vent and to develop their own group agenda, issues or focus, and time- and subject-management approach. Sometimes, this initially **blank-slate, or "no-text,"** approach is critical to developing trust, collaboration, and eventually EDR. As dispute-resolution communities become effective, practitioners can guide no-text events into one-text EDR efforts.

If participants have facilitation skills, formal facilitation may not be necessary, but meeting managers usually call for facilitation at agenda-less meetings. In deciding to hold an agenda-less meeting, EDR practitioners should consider whether starting a resolution effort without an agenda might reduce tensions or, if creativity would be useful, whether the range of options and group cohesion will improve through brainstorming.

In situations when tensions are high, or situations in which highly structured negotiation or mediation is taking place, EDR practitioners may use a **caucus-and-plenary** style. A **caucus** is usually a meeting among like-minded people, often sharing similar values around a dispute. A **plenary** is a meeting of everyone involved in the dispute-resolution effort. Using a variable caucus-and-plenary pattern, practitioners can convene the whole group when needed for group norming, sharing information, celebrating settlements, etc. Alternatively, practitioners can separate disputants into caucuses for small-group deliberations and the formulation of offers or counter-offers. Sometimes practitioners combine the caucus-and-plenary approach with a one-text method to develop an acceptable resolution.

Another meeting and interactive form is the "**walking caucus,**" which allows people to circulate around a room to different subject-matter "stations." In this method, participants can gain information from a subject-matter expert, discuss interests with other interested people, and offer opinions and options for resolution. Sometimes, practitioners ask people to array themselves along an arc or in a line to indicate their support or resistance to a resolution proposal — this "voting with your feet" approach is called a walking caucus, too.

All types of meetings may be useful in EDR work, depending on how the EDR practitioner wishes to address the dispute. These are the characteristics to take into consideration:

Highly Structured	←——→	Highly Flexible
Detailed rules and norms (e.g., Roberts Rules of Order)		Simple rules
Defined schedule		Open schedule (Maybe just end-point)
Limited participants (May have few principals who wield power in front of an audience)		Participation varies (May be permeable to many)

Whether highly structured or highly flexible, leaders or EDR practitioners may choose to direct the meetings or have them facilitated:

Highly Structured	←——→		Highly Flexible
Business meeting	Working lunch	Brainstorming sessions
Public forum	Open house	Ad hoc meeting
Working meeting	Issue dialog	Charette
Public hearing	Open team mtg.	Beer and pretzels session
Group e-mails	Blog	Chat room

EDR practitioners should choose their meeting type and style based on desired dispute outcomes. The wrong type may alienate disputants and exacerbate the dispute. Some styles are more effective in early dispute stages and less effective later.

Key factors in meeting design include decisions about participants, location, agenda, length, facilitation, sponsorship, leadership, record keeping and sharing, security, and timing. The greater the number and intensity of values conflicts among the disputants, the more formal meetings often have to be and the more negotiation often has to occur in advance to gain agreement and commitment to the meeting design.

An EDR practitioner may have to spend months working among the disputants to arrange the first in a series of dispute-resolution meetings. Many times, after beginning with considerable formality, the meeting design evolves to an informal style. The one exception to this shift is if a formal "signing ceremony" is required to publicly "seal the deal" and gain long-term commitment to action.

Using Methods from Traditional Communities

Cultures from all over the world offer ideas for EDR methods; most involve third-party interveners, peacemakers, reconciliation methods, and means of dispute communication and debate. Some involve mock or ritual combat.

Communities of tradition often have EDR methods that work well within their cultural context. For example, the traditional New England town hall meeting is classic American democratic meetings style in which debate and votes are used to set public priorities, make decisions, and reinforce shared culture. American Indians, Pacific Islanders, and Alaska Natives all have some traditional form of peacemakers, dispute-resolving cultural leaders, and dispute-resolution methods.

EDR practitioners may want to ask among disputants and caring onlookers if they have any traditional methods for consideration. At least as a method, some of these approaches are transferable to other cultures, although the cultural context will always change and may influence success. For example, mock combat involving shoving and ritual club fighting between two "champions," as practiced among some Central American Indian tribes, would be interesting and entertaining to a group that was attempting to settle an environmental dispute in New York City, but it would not likely substitute effectively for a court-ordered mediation.

Many people have heard of the **Samoan Circle**[18] technique in which, during times of high tension, disputants self-convene to a central place. Usually

---

[18] www.peopleandparticipation.net

a table is set up in the middle of a room, and people arrange chairs in a circle around the table. The symbolism of the circle is that no one is better or more influential than anyone else is. No one conducts the meeting, but one-by-one, disputants and caring onlookers come to the central table and, speaking to no one in particular, saying what is on their minds. People speak until no one else has anything to say, and then the Samoan Circle is over. The intent of a Samoan Circle is to achieve tension de-escalation so that other resolution efforts can move forward.

Community leaders or EDR practitioners may also convene similar **"support circles"** to help disputants reconcile or achieve a settlement. Disputants sit dispersed throughout the circle, while caring onlookers come forward to the central table and explain why resolution is so important for them and for the community. Support speakers may offer options for resolution but do not support one disputant over another.

Other methods adopted ostensibly from American Indian traditions are the "**white feather**" or "**medicine staff**" approaches. Similar to the Samoan Circle, disputants sit in a circle but face inward so they are able to see one another, and they agree to remain in their places during the exercise. A leader announces the topic, and the white feather, medicine staff (or another object) begins to pass around the circle. With the white feather, people usually remain seated. With the medicine staff, they usually rise. Only

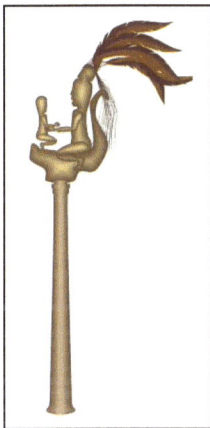

the person holding the object speaks. Sometimes, particularly in times of high tension, the group agrees in advance to only speak to the leader. The object continues to travel around the circle until no one has anything else to say. Sometimes this method leads to resolution, and sometimes, like the Samoan Circle, it leads to tension de-escalation to enable other resolution methods.

In Alaska, I participated in a traditional reconciliation meeting and ceremony between the Forest Service and Tlingit Indians. We began the settlement of a serious, long-standing dispute over the ownership and burial of Indian skeletal remains by having a meal of traditional foods, hosted by the native clans involved and **potlatch** style. We then held a ceremony in which a Forest Service leader, who had been carefully coached by native elders, stood up and said he had come as a "deer" (the native symbol for gentleness and he said, "Our conflict has no more weight than this feather and drifts away as lightly."

Tlingit clan leaders then rose and agreed that the dispute was over. Their spokesperson said, "This night our (hand carved, wooden) clan hats are holding hands with the Eagle Hat (meaning the federal government and Forest Service)." Having been acquainted with the dispute for about a decade, I felt touched to tears by the simplicity and effectiveness of the ceremony and my gratitude for its use.

I am in awe of the Medicine Wheel site on the west side of the Big Horn Mountains in Wyoming. Built by paleo-indians, the site sits high on a ridge overlooking hundreds of square miles of ridges, valleys, and plains. The Medicine Wheel itself is made of rocks and small boulders arranged in a spoked-wheel shape. Many people visit the site, including modern-day American Indians, who often leave small mementoes and offerings.

I recently read about a **Medicine Wheel mediation model**. Apparently, Indians in Vancouver, WA use it to deal with disputes. Leaders create a wheel shape and participants move through its four directions. Starting with the east, they first examine their spiritual connections to each other, their community, and the resources. Then they turn south and experience and discuss their emotions and the condition of their hearts. Next, they turn west, discuss the physical reality of the dispute, and offer respect to the Creator. Then, they turn north and engage their intellect and creativity to deal with the dispute. Finally, they move to the center of the wheel where they make decisions about resolution actions.[19]

EDR practitioners may find that groups or individuals resist the use of traditional First Peoples methods for dispute resolution because of racial bias or a fear reaction to trying something potentially embarrassing. Some patient work with these individuals is usually effective. I can usually get them to go along with the effort by asking them to "just give it a try, and if this doesn't work or you really dislike it, we'll try something else."

Additional problems can occur when EDR leaders ask participants to accept the traditional knowledge or **aboriginal wisdom** of American natives and give it the same kind of respect and consideration as scientific knowledge. Aboriginal wisdom often strikes some participants as farfetched or hard to comprehend because of cultural differences. Although I see less of this than 25 years ago, scientists trained formally in the scientific method and immersed in their profession may also find aboriginal wisdom off-putting because it is anecdotal and often conveyed as stories. Leaders should consult with participants about their comfort with both aboriginal techniques and aboriginal wisdom before using either extensively in EDR.

Traditional-communities are rich territory for finding good dispute-resolution techniques because they often deal with disputants holistically, engaging conflicts fully as people and within the context of their culture and community. The lack of official sanction or cultural context for them, and their apparent strangeness for many participants, may limit their value or rule them out as unacceptable to many participants. EDR practitioners should always consider these realities before employing them, and practitioners should probably try them out at small scale before employing them more widely or at large scale.

---

[19] Huber, M. "Mediation Around the Medicine Wheel," *Mediation Quarterly*, 1993.10(4), 355-365

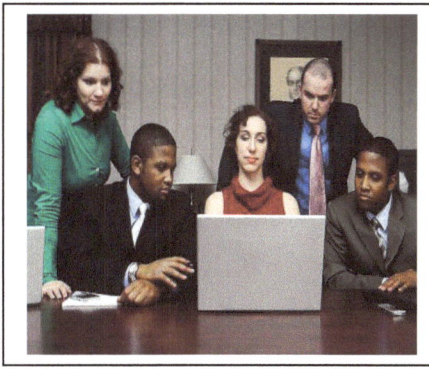

Towards Collaboration

I have a passion for building collaborative relationships and groups. I have given several examples throughout this book of collaboration in different forms, including structural changes such as those we developed mutually between Douglas County, Oregon; the Umpqua National Forest; and among nine agencies for the restoration of Diamond Lake.

Collaboration means individuals and groups working together to achieve outcomes that are mutually determined and mutually beneficial. **Collaborative groups, panels and teams** transcend ideas about power coalitions — groups that exist to achieve an objective and then "divide up" the results most often encountered in business or legislative settings. Unlike power coalitions, collaborative entities often achieve higher-order outcomes in the public interest rather than more parochial, self-rewarding ends. Collaborative entities often have highly developed understandings of each member's values, strong norms for respecting those values, methods for sustaining trust, and protocols for effective communication and EDR.

Currently, academics and practitioner have begun to use the term "collaboration" as they once did the term "public participation."[20] In that context, readers should not be confused by the new twist. However, the evolution in terms from "public participation" to "collaboration" is a positive one because it speaks to the desired outcome more accurately—intense, values-exchanging involvement of citizens in environmental decision-making and management. So, collaboration is at once a public engagement philosophy, an articulation of desired outcome, a set of practices, and a specific design for a group.

 EDR practitioners might be asked, or find it advantageous, to achieve collaboration among disputants. While collaboration can take many forms, EDR often has to be effective before collaboration is possible. The power in collaboration is the ability to take on controversial issues and opportunities and to make progress, to solve "wicked" problems. If disputes go unmanaged or unresolved, collaboration will likely fail or focus only on non-controversial opportunities.

Groups follow a certain progression on their way from first convening to eventual collaboration. As collaboration grows, participants have to "move" from focusing on dispute stories to consenting to working together and developing more supportive relationships; then they move to setting goals together to enable separate but complimentary work; then to carrying out joint operations based on individual efforts; and finally to collaborating and literally working side by side to achieve a common good.

---

[20] *Special Issue on Collaborative Public Management.* O'Leary, R., Bingham, L. B., Gerard, C. Public Administration Review. 2006. (66) 6 Supp.

Some participants condition their involvement in a collaborative group on the idea that collaboration is simply another form of coalition building. These folks remain committed only to the degree that they feel their values and interests benefit. This "power coalition" value is one that may come up during values discussions, and EDR practitioners must be ready to deal with the idea's implications. The idea implies that these participants will likely attempt to control the other participants by offering to quit whenever their interests go unmet.

Since collaboration requires finding common ground and common purpose, the group must discuss "power coalition" and other polarizing behaviors, place them in context with the purposes of collaboration. They must also produce agreed-to norms to handle the behaviors if they should appear.

Fundamentally, collaboration is the combination of corporate or public-agency interdisciplinary teamwork and advisory group concepts, and it extends them to work with dispute-resolution communities. Those who promote collaboration hope that it will improve decisions and resolve disputes by binding representatives into a rational process that is supported by mediators, facilitators, and other experts.

Collaboration sometimes under-performs expectations because it lacks adequate legal underpinnings, may mesh poorly with environmental-management and public decision-making authorities and processes (such as those associated with the National Environmental Policy Act), and is difficult or impossible to apply at any large geographic scale (say larger than a land type association or sub-section, see Chapter 4 of Theory and Principles) because of the enormous scope of involving potential collaborators meaningfully. Social media such as Facebook may offer some potential for engaging large groups in collaborative efforts over broad geographic scales.

In addition, most collaborative groups have the rights to assess, analyze, discuss, and advise but not to control outcomes or prevail; thus, they have no power to implement agreements or actions and must depend on others for that. When collaborative group members discover that their role is largely advisory, they often lose interest, and some may exit to pursue litigation or political means to express their values. This is especially so if the group falls into intractable disputes and power struggles, if those people with the authority to implement agreements chose to modify or ignore them, or if further lengthy decision-making efforts are conducted.

Many people using collaborative groups also recognize that, unless practitioners and facilitators build EDR focus and methods into the process, the group is likely to gridlock when full-blown conflicts appear.

Media

EDR practitioners should understand that the media, **electronic and print, broadcast and narrowcast**, could be allies in dispute resolution. However, typically, they are not.

Most media promote disputes in their coverage by reporting positioning, power plays, and full-blown conflicts. The media often follow the practice of "if it bleeds, it leads." This means that sensational stories about distress, scandal, anarchy, and catastrophe get top billing and often emphasize conflict or loss.

Investigative reporters often thrive on discovering "the dirt" and reporting it. Surprise interviews, called "ambushes," of EDR practitioners and participants can happen.

Editorial pages and talking heads or pundits exist to communicate opposing positions, including those held by editors, media owners, and prominent officials.

However, if EDR practitioners develop relationships with the media in an open, careful, and respectful fashion, media can be a deciding factor in developing dispute management and resolution approaches. My approach to media has always been respectful, but when working with significant controversy and conflict, I am unusually careful because poorly stated or out-of-context quotes have great potential for alienating disputants.

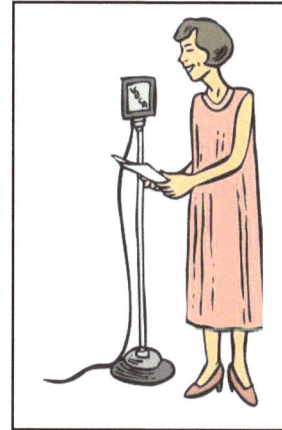

I start with the **editor or editorial board** of the newspaper, and with the management staff at electronic media. If I know of other influential media, which today would include **bloggers**, I would contact them as well. However, I do not approach them with a "sales job."

My purpose in visiting them is simply to let them know what is going on and what approach I plan to take to address the dispute. I cover timing and method, likely participants and allies. I discuss story possibilities. I let them know I will try to conduct the EDR effort in an open manner and that I will ask participants to be open as well.

I ask that they try to cover the effort in-depth, but I express that I know feature stories and Sunday-supplement coverage may be cost-prohibitive. I offer to work with them to give short progress reports to help make their job easier.

At times, if I feel the resolution process could benefit, I produce a multi-page insert to the paper or a feature videotape for public airing to provide full coverage of an issue or conflict. This insert or tape portrays "just the facts, ma'am" to the public, and at the same time it tries to cover the subject fully and in terms just about anyone can grasp.

As dispute tensions rise, particularly in situations of full-blown conflict headed towards crisis, I formulate and practice talking points, both factual and anecdotal — in case media folks ambush me. This preparation is also useful for routine media contacts, which usually occur in increasing numbers as disputes escalate.

Communications

Like all communications, dispute communications fall into two broad categories: verbal and non-verbal. Verbal communication involves the exchange of symbols and is usually oral, written, or sign language. Non-verbal communication involves the development of nuance or impression through body movement, position or condition, speech intonation, facial expressions, clothing style, distances or height differences among participants, pictures or other decorations, lighting, or setting elements such as location, furnishings, and the symbolic presence of other people or objects.

The importance of understanding both verbal and non-verbal communications in dispute situations is extremely important. Psychological phenomena, such as transference and resistance, and cultural and personal differences over the meaning of words and symbols tend to heighten strife around values conflicts. During dispute escalation, tensions rise, and effective communications becomes ever more essential; yet, communications tend to break down as the frequency, nature, and content of the communication gets more constrained and potentially alienating.

EDR practitioners need not be communications experts, but they should have access to communications expertise. EDR work requires a careful blend of verbal and non-verbal communications, and an understanding of when certain methods and means contribute differently to dispute resolution at different stages.

Verbal Communications Techniques

Verbal communications may be written or unwritten, although all involve the exchange of symbols between two or more people. Written communications can be hard copy or electronic. Unwritten communications involve speaking or sign language, such as American Sign Language or operational hand signals used in construction or military activities.

Written communications come in many forms from letters to encyclopedias, from chalk letters on a sidewalk to skywriting, from a simple newsletter to the *New York Times*.

Many forms of written communication have the inherent advantages of clarity, legibility, durability, reproducibility, portability, and low cost. You may not be able to communicate hard copy as quickly or as widely as electronic material, but hard copy has the advantage of greater durability. Overall, written communications have the disadvantage of being single-direction communications that struggle to share values.

Their effectiveness also suffers when writers assume a common capacity among their readers for reading and understanding. They may also exacerbate disputes by communicating positions or accusations.

EDR practitioners should select the written verbal communications most likely to add to their success. They cannot rely solely on written verbal communications to help address disputes.

Unwritten verbal communications can include many actions:
- Speeches to thousands of people or one-on-one dialogs
- Gossip mongering at the supermarket or expert testimony before a court or Congress
- Singing in the shower or arias sung at the Metropolitan Opera
- Casual gestures to emphasize a point at a cocktail party or a political dissertation delivered in American Sign Language to the deaf community.

Oral and sign language communications have the advantage of often being concurrent with non-verbal communications, which means that audience understanding and meaning may be greatly improved. Many times, oral and sign language communications enable values sharing and relationship building. EDR workers can be trained in "effective listening" techniques that reassure people that they are being listened to and heard.

Oral and sign language messages are not durable, reproducible, or portable unless practitioners transcribe them into a document or capture them electronically. Unless speakers provide clear communications to participants, they may not convey the meaningful messages they intend. Many people leave EDR efforts with very different understanding and interpretations of oral or sign language messages.

EDR practitioners should select the unwritten verbal communications most likely to add to their success. They cannot rely solely on unwritten verbal communications to help address disputes.

Non-Verbal Communications Techniques

Non-verbal communications involves the development of nuance or impression. I have often heard that non-verbal communication comprises about 80 percent of all communications. Therefore, EDR practitioners must understand the importance and value of effective nonverbal messaging.

Body movement during speeches or in reaction to the communications of others can be critical in convincing audiences of trustworthiness, sincerity, commitment, and credibility. Body movement includes body position or change that conveys focus, interest, and acceptance or rejection of messages from others.

It also includes facial expressions that constitute a strong and more precise communications. In recent years, EDR practitioners have used techniques for "micro-expression" reading that assists facial-movement interpreters to grasp the true feelings of their subjects.

Along with speech volume, intonation and speed are used to condition oral communications. In settings where sign language is used, body movement, facial expression, and additional symbols substitute for volume, intonation, and speed.

Volume considerations are important to assure audiences can actually hear speakers but without the sound blasting them out of their chairs. Intonation and speed patterns are so critical that differences can actually reverse the meaning of words or phrases, even turning questions into statements or vice versa. They are also critical to convincing audiences of trustworthiness, sincerity, commitment, and credibility of speakers — and they are a principal means for motivating audiences.

Clothing style, components, color, and accessories convey important messages about the wearer. I am no fashion expert, but EDR practitioners must understand the effects of such clothing as police uniforms and accessories such as guns and batons on audiences. In this sense, dress can be either intimidating or reassuring. They must also understand the impacts and values of professional business dress, informal dress, or "down-dress." One causes practitioners and speakers to stand out, and the other causes them to blend in. Depending on the dispute stage and conditions, visibility and separateness may be important to build legitimacy and credibility; but under other circumstances, EDR practitioners may wish to blend in to build trust and reduce tensions.

Other considerations, particularly in meetings or during confrontations, include the distance between participants, how and where the participants are distributed spatially, and whether one group or individual are located higher than others.

People separated by considerable distance tend to feel less threatened than when their disputants are close to them. Therefore, when tensions are high, making sure distances are consistent with people's desire for safety is important. Event arrangers may want to arrange for barriers or security people to restrain aggressive movements sufficiently. As tensions decline, making sure people are able to approach and mingle is equally important because it is part of the context for forming a sense of shared space, interest, and community.

In situations of low or moderate tension, I try to space people so that power coalitions are broken up or mixed together. Sometimes I assign seats. Sometimes I distribute neutral parties or agency people around a room or a space, interspersing them within groups or power coalitions. Sometimes I use teambuilding, group-cohesion icebreakers, or a technique like a "walking caucus" to create movement and distribution and start dialog.

If I find that one group or an individual has literally "taken the high ground," I will usually figure out a way to reduce or eliminate that advantage. For example, it is common for presenters and decision makers in public hearings to be high up on a stage or a dais looking and talking down to the audience. This is fine for comedians, musicians, and actors, but in disputes, it tends to increase alienation.

To avoid the "high ground-talking down" problem and to help deal with some related participant-distribution issues, I once convinced the federal Subsistence Board in Alaska to take their seats throughout the audience, identify themselves, and conduct the public hearing with just the recorder at the front of the room. I also asked the person giving testimony to turn towards the audience to address the Board along with their neighbors. Everyone was on the same level and part of a community of interest and place. It worked very well to diffuse a tense, racially charged situation.

Another consideration is whether to videotape or otherwise record events. At times, this practice intimidates people and may prevent acting out by dissident groups or individuals. Other times, it serves to record testimony, values communications, and decisions or agreements.

Lighting is another consideration. Visually impaired people require certain light levels to participate effectively, and low lights effectively bar them from participation. However, bright lights can be equally intimidating for participants because the glare contributes to their discomfort and adds to alienation.

Practitioners should consider other aspects of the setting for their effectiveness in EDR work. Location is important for both its physical feasibility and its symbolic importance. The "wrong place" may not just be physically inaccessible to some participants; it can also be defined as representative of the dispute or too advantageous to one disputant or another.

Once at the location, furnishings, surface colors, odor and the symbolic presence of other people or objects can be important. Furnishings can work to help make people comfortable, distribute them efficiently and effectively, and promote organization and activities. Elements to consider include the quality and comfort of tables and chairs and their distribution around the space.

Surface colors affect people's comfort and behavior. For example, jails have "weak rooms" painted pink because violent males are physically weaker when incarcerated there. Neutral or "cool" colors may lessen tensions for some individuals and groups.

What is hanging on the walls as art or political expression can be important too. For example, holding a meeting with the Jewish Defense League in a room with a swastika probably requires an explanation such as its use as a symbol by American Indians. A picture or video of a herd of animals will have a calming effect on onlookers, according to environmental psychologists.

Symbols can make a difference. Having clergy, pregnant women, or children participating can calm tensions. The presence of important or respected people, even if they are not direct participants, can assist in this regard as well. Practitioners should evaluate cultural symbols like the American flag or the Ten Commandments for the appropriateness of their use in conducting EDR.

Simulations and Games

EDR practitioners have a wide variety of simulations and games available to them to use for reference and to educate disputants and other participants. With the permission of the participants, practitioners can use games like those discussed in Chapter 8 of Theory and Principles to help people understand the implications of zero-sum and non-zero-sum approaches to disputes.

Chapter 8 of Theory and Principles discusses **zero-sum games such as tit-for-tat, tit-for-double-tat, Prisoners' Dilemma and Gambler's Dilemma**. Games tending towards greater cooperation, such as **Paratroopers' Dilemma, Forester's Dilemma, and Elders' Dilemma**, are also useful. Practitioners can adjust rewards and scores to encourage pure cooperation to simulate "feel" for participants. **"Super gaming"** can add additional insight into the participant's strategies and tactics that might be hidden otherwise in the basic games.

Sometimes, **role-play and role-reversal play** are useful for both educational and barrier-reducing purposes. In role- or role-reversal play, disputants are encouraged to play the part of other people in a scripted session that explores the dispute and the values people hold around the dispute. Scripted work can then lead to further talk with participants staying "in character." Role-reversal play specifically places disputants in values positions opposite of their normal stance. This kind of simulation often reveals how limited some positions are, how much disputants understand one another, and how flexible or inflexible values held by the players can be.

In some cases, **reality simulations** can be useful. In this method, a neutral panel hears and reflects on the positions, rationales, proposed strategies, and possible tactics of the disputants for handling the dispute. Once the disputants have presented their ideas and arguments, the panel is able to provide insightful feedback about each disputant's effectiveness and persuasiveness. EDR practitioners should try to avoid the appearance of a "**moot court**," or courtroom simulation that is likely to increase tension rather than reduce it.

Other Important Techniques

Practitioners may want to develop the means to communicate quickly to, and among, many participants. Some useful techniques include **telephone trees, teleconferences, videoconferences, e-mail lists, key contact lists, chat rooms, blogs, e-videos, and web-casts.** Practitioners should select the technique that best suits the participants and their technological capability. For example, many people are moving to Web-based communications and dialoguing, but about one-half of all Americans lack the ability to access these opportunities. Thus, practitioners may have to settle for low-tech solutions for communicating in some disputes.

Common monitoring protocols and shared databases tend to bring disputants and other participants together for information acquisition and interpretation efforts. Agency and non-governmental organization people can play a beneficial role in using scientific knowledge to help develop protocols, store information, and standardize reporting schemes to benefit the dispute-resolution community.

To common monitoring protocols and shared database efforts, EDR practitioners can add **citizen or volunteer science and management**. In this technique, citizens play a role in the data acquisition and interpretation efforts. Usually, scientists guide the work and agency staff assures that citizen volunteers follow protocols properly. This technique works to bring members of the dispute-resolution community together and can build long-term dispute-resolution skills and capability. Making it citizen- and community-based creates accommodation for the occasional turnover of agency people.

EDR practitioners and event organizers may choose to use **visuals, graphics, power point, on-screen text building** (web or one-location). Almost any part of an EDR effort can benefit from good visuals and records. The more EDR participants feel that the content of the visual materials represent their values, the more credible those materials will be for them. **Geographic Information Systems and other map and database visual aides and 3-D models** also complement EDR efforts by putting information in front of participants, permitting interpretation, and allowing option testing.

Practitioners can use **social impact assessment and evaluation**[21] to determine the effects of proposals, including EDR proposals, on potentially affected interests. When issues concern environmental justice, practitioners may find that **civil rights and minority-impact assessments and evaluations** can also be helpful.

Reviewing **polls, surveys, editorials, letters to the editor, interviews, and ethnographic and oral histories** serve to inform the EDR effort with information about social trends and public values preferences. EDR practitioners should make sure polls and experts use scientifically defensible methods (e.g., an adequate sample from a sufficient universe) to conduct polls and surveys. If participants perceive bias in the method or results, the legitimacy and credibility of the EDR practitioners and the overall effort will be undermined.

---

[21] www.socialimpactassessment.net

103

Editorials, letters to the editor, interviews, and oral histories are all anecdotal information useful for their ability to convey historic, contextual, and values-preference information. Formal histories and ethnographies are expert peer-reviewed information sources that convey factual material but offer less insight regarding individual values.

This information can be invaluable, but practitioners should not attempt to mingle it with survey and poll results, or claim that the information represents widely held values or experiences.

Practitioners may find that **social/psychological values-in-conflict testing, values mapping and charting**[22] **and displaying disputes** for participants are good ways to assess conflicts using scientific methods and the present the results verbally and visually. This can also involve developing and displaying **values or care fabrics** that show hierarchies and connections among values held by participants. These methods are particularly good for people who see the value in scientific analysis of conflict and who learn visually. When practitioners use such displays interactively with participants, they enable improved communications and focus on participants' values and EDR options and ideas.

Other sources of information about values and options include **nominal, Delphi, and focus groups**, and **expert or cross-sectional roundtables**[23]. Practitioners employing these techniques should be ready to explain the technique, train participants, and enforce rules and deadlines to make them effective.

The Delphi process uses panels of experts or knowledgeable people not known to one another. Practitioners present them with a question or series of questions from the dispute community. The individual Delphi group members' answers get circulated among the whole group until the group reaches a consensus. Practitioners share this consensus opinion with the dispute-resolution community as expert information useful for EDR.

Depending on topic and desired results, practitioners populate focus groups and expert or cross-sectional roundtables to provide similar opinion results. While these techniques may have less value as expert or scientific knowledge, they can provide excellent information regarding values or options. When practitioners convene a cross-sectional roundtable, they select the people who will sit at the table because they represent specific groups or values systems.

An unusual variation on the Delphi approach is called **Dialog in the Dark**. In this technique, blind people lead sighted people through a zero-light, maze environment.

---

[22] Public Value Mapping off Science Outcomes:: Theory and Method. Barry Bozeman. Center for Science, Policy, & Outcomes. A Project of Columbia University. Washington, DC 20005
[23] www.fhwa.dot.gov/REPORTS/PITTD/smlgroup

Dialog in the Dark is used as a means to educate the sighted and create an experiential dialog. Effective listening is used to promote better understanding among the participants and Delphi methods are used to illicit expert opinions and ideas from sighted participants. A similar approach to dialog could be embraced for other disputants in situations where their life experiences differed greatly from one another.

Conducting walking or street surveys, or "spitin' and whittlin'," refer to deliberate, casual visits with individuals and groups who are part of the dispute community. Leaders may choose to spend considerable time doing this work to build trust and understanding. Sometimes, practitioners establish a **trap line** process whereby they make frequent drop-in visits to individuals or at certain locations to keep the flow of information and understanding at high levels. Practitioners also sometimes establish **trading posts,** or locations that they visit at established times to meet and interact with people such as country stores or bars.

Tactics

During EDR efforts, powerful supporters should consider establishing an **open door** and an **"any place, any time"** meeting approach. Combined with **fishbowl** public deliberations, these tactics will go a long way towards building public trust in the EDR effort.

Practitioners may want to employ some tactics, or encourage participants to employ them, to help increase the potential for EDR success. Early in an effort, practitioners should encourage disputants and other participants to **"vent"** (give voice or expression to) their frustrations, fears, and concerns. Practitioners may want to use mental health or counseling professionals to assist participants with venting. If venting is not encouraged, key values and emotions may go unexpressed for a long time and ultimately undermine the EDR effort and increase the potential for recycling. Practitioners may find venting a good way to get an initial read on the intensity of the dispute and the values held by the participants.

A useful public process to promote venting is called a **soapbox session** in which people give speeches about their fears, frustrations, etc. to the larger dispute community. To promote a sense of safety for everyone, behavioral norms are agreed to in advance (such as no name calling, no interruptions, and no threats). The speaker usually faces the community and speaks for a set amount of time. A moderator or facilitator usually assists the dispute community.

As practitioners move EDR efforts forward, they may choose to work with disputants to **"delink"** them from working directly on disputed issues and focus them on building effective working relationships. Once delinked, practitioners can guide participants through exercises intended to reduce inter-personal conflicts and to develop group norms or rules before returning to the environmental dispute itself.

Also early in EDR efforts, practitioners and participants must describe or **frame** the dispute and its inherent issues. Participants have to affirm what it is they are working on. Later, as new information comes forward, group cohesion develops, and communications improves, participants may **reframe** issues collaboratively. At this stage, oftentimes **key issues** emerge and many items thought important early on drop away or participants designate them for later, sequential treatment.

As framing and reframing occur, practitioners can also encourage participants to reframe, or **re-image,** their perceptions of disputants and other participants. For example, if de-escalation of blame is important to EDR success, practitioners should focus on helping participants acknowledge that disputants did not act with personal malice or in ways that reflect unconscious characteristics. A simple transformational approach could mean that practitioners ask disputants and other participants to:

- **Describe one good thing about a disputant**
- **Describe one good thing about themselves**
- **Restate the EDR goal and how they will feel about reaching that goal**
- **Reaffirm their dedication to EDR and resolving the key issues they consider important**

Participants may experience embarrassment based on past perceptions held towards others, by their past actions or statements, or from statements made about them. EDR practitioners should look for effective ways to allow participants to **save face**. Otherwise, participants may exit the EDR effort or the dispute may escalate without apparent explanation. **Saving face** is particularly important with some cultures and in situations where there is significant power asymmetry.

Along with saving face, practitioners should look for **patterns** among the disputants and participants. These patterns may reflect past dispute recycling ("we always settle it this way") or they may suggest efficient, time-proven approaches, particularly if the addition of a few new ideas or methods make resolution more effective.

Sometimes, past patterns include **sidebar or shadow contacts** between disputants. These are off-the-record contacts outside more formal techniques. Practitioners should make sure that, although initial discussions can be sidebar or shadow efforts, any settlements or attempts at resolution get brought to the full group as soon as feasible. Fomenters will enhance group trust and credibility if they communicate about sidebars or shadow contacts and their subjects to all participants as soon as they begin. However, even with early acknowledgement, some participants will be skeptical, and practitioners must make sure there is enough time to consider and ratify any resolution proposals.

EDR practitioners may find themselves in situations where disputants are willing to enter into **reciprocal agreements and structured settlements.** These may be simple tit-for-tat or horse-trading agreements/settlements. They also may include time-discontinuous agreements wherein one disputant gets an immediate concession or action and the other accepts deferred consideration. In the structural sense, these have to be legally binding

agreements, but more importantly, in the compositional sense, the agreements have to be un-coerced, explicit, and written down. Otherwise, long-term trust may be lost and disputes may escalate or recycle.

During meetings or other community events, practitioners or facilitators may want to **appeal to participants' sense of fair play or higher values,** or they might **reaffirm event rules** to reduce the intensity of verbal conflict and to reaffirm commitments to successful EDR.

Sometimes, in highly charged situations, practitioners may want to begin an event by choosing who speaks or acts first in an impartial way. **Coin flips, tossing dice, high-low card, casting lots, "rock-paper-scissors"** or other random selection methods may be a good choice. These techniques impart a sense of fun and symbolically emphasize the impartiality of the EDR practitioners.

Leaders may have to impose **group sanctions or disputant separation** on uncooperative participants in order to reduce dispute intensity and inappropriate behavior, and the choice to apply sanctions or separations should not be undertaken lightly. If leaders undertake these methods, they must show the dispute-resolution community how the sanction or separation enables EDR. For example, leaders may call for a separation to help participants de-link from the dispute details and focus on desired success, or the leaders may be using a plenary-and-caucus meeting technique and will have built separations into their effort.

Practitioners may want to orient event participants by talking to actions that reduce intensity. For example, practitioners may encourage participants to consider:

- Walking away or moving to another activity and returning later
- Asking disputants to please stop aggressive actions or speech
- Asking disputants to allow open communications
- Making an accommodation or arrangement with an disputant to work towards EDR success
- Sharing resources or opportunities

One form of sanction is for a dispute-resolution community to use the **election process** to remove incumbents or deny office to candidates who foment or exacerbate disputes or who display bias toward one disputant or another. The community can act through either the **general election or a recall vote.** Long-term EDR is served better if the electorate understands that the rationale for eliminating an incumbent or denying a candidate rests on the urgency of, and impetus toward, dispute resolution, not partisanship politics or single-issue polarization.

Techniques to Precipitate Crisis

Practitioners and others who might consider using techniques that precipitate crisis should remember the discussion about how public land managers use fire to reduce fuels to prevent a major, highly destructive fire. In addition, remember the medical admonition that applies well to EDR: "First, do no harm."

If they are not careful, people using techniques that precipitate crisis can cause great harm to relationships and needlessly perpetuate disputes.

Personalizing a dispute means to carry the issues to the person or people most responsible for the existing condition, folding them into the process so they can influence others or can resolve the dispute. When the personalization effort begins, these targeted folks are generally not yet a party to the EDR effort, but they may be standing on the periphery without an active role. Personalizing a dispute can be face-to-face or through the media or other intermediaries.

To be effective as a dispute-resolution technique, personalizing cannot be coercive or disrespectful. If practitioners or others use personalizing in a blaming, coercive, or disrespectful manner, the dispute will escalate along the personal distress pathway, and the person or group will display a fright response.

If practitioners present the issues embedded in a dispute as a problem or as an opportunity, and moreover convey that the targeted person or group has responsibility for or a significant role in its resolution, chances are high that the technique will be successful. Practitioners also usually present what will happen if the targeted person or group does not act. Before the presentation, practitioners should work to understand the values held by the targeted person or group so that they can present issues and abatement proposals with those values in mind.

Rapid accumulation is the use of media, other communication means, and direct actions such as civil disobedience before various media "lenses" to develop public understanding of a dispute and its possible resolution. When EDR practitioners use rapid accumulation, it is with the intention to precipitate a crisis at low levels and is not meant to be favorable to any particular disputant or values. Generally, practitioners appeal to the public and public decision-makers to prevent unacceptable loss or to seize an important opportunity.

"Sunlight is said to be the best of disinfectants" wrote Justice Louis Brandeis. **Sunlight or sunshine** refers to creating public scrutiny on a problem condition or an opportunity that might otherwise be concealed. This technique removes the condition or opportunity from obscurity and highlights it for public consideration. If EDR practitioners or leaders adopt a sunshine approach, they should avoid blaming or shaming and should work to prevent the release of confidential information, particularly business information.

"Twisting slowly, slowly in the wind" technique refers to an H.R. Haldeman phrase from the Watergate scandal: isolating and publicly punishing someone for disloyalty or poor performance. In this case, the technique refers to raising and examining a key issue or past action without attributing it to anyone. Once the key issue is raised, EDR participants are invited to discuss the issue publicly. Similar to the sunshine technique, this technique uses public scrutiny to add pressure for change to an otherwise obscure problem or opportunity without personalizing blame.

In some cases, people may find themselves in a situation where their disputant has, or acts as if they have, greater positional or tacit power — at least in a narrow context. The person with lesser power may consider taking the dispute into a larger context to create greater symmetry using such "checks and balances" methods as appeals to the courts, requests for intervention by investigative or watchdog agencies, or demands for legislative oversight. This action can mean high cost and low satisfaction for both disputants. However, there is another technique called **shaking the table**. This technique signals the disputant with greater apparent power that the dispute is about to escalate towards a situation of greater power symmetry and higher cost**s**

Picture a chess game in which one disputant is sight impaired (has lesser power), and the other disputant is taking advantage of the impairment by moving pieces several times before settling on a "best" tactical position. The more powerful disputant is engaging in this behavior even though the game's rules and supposed personal commitment by the more a powerful player should be preventing it.

The sight-impaired disputant could call "foul" to a judge, crying shame and escalating the dispute, probably permanently harming relationships and ending the game. Or the sight-impaired player can extend her leg and bump one of the table's legs, thereby shaking the table and toppling the chess pieces.

The chaos of the pieces on the board and the need for cooperation to replace them in their pre-topple places creates a crisis-precipitating opportunity. As the disputants are collaboratively putting the pieces back on the game board, the table-shaker can say quietly, "As we continue this game, maybe we should review the rules. I would like to make sure we both understand them. Before I knocked the chess pieces down, I was thinking about lodging a complaint against you for shuffling your pieces, but I really do not want to make a big fuss over nothing. What do you think?" The key to this technique is to understand that:

- Minor, well-designed, "shaking-the-table" chaos can change the playing field temporarily
- Although it may be frustrating, as long as the change is not threatening, the disruption on the playing field creates a mini-crisis and an opportunity for cooperative recovery actions
- Then, the cooperative action allows the discussion of issues abatement with constructive behavioral change.

Brinksmanship has the potential to precipitate crisis effectively, but it also has many risks. As Fredrich Neitzsche (1844-1900) wrote, *"When you gaze long into the abyss, the abyss also gazes into you."* Brinksmanship refers to taking an issue or situation "to the brink of the abyss" in order to confront disputants and powerful decision-makers with the specter of a crisis.

Used well, brinksmanship gets attention directed toward serious problems or compelling opportunities at just the right time. But, many times brinksmanship is ill-timed and a crisis occurs with no controls, or sometimes interests not normally parties to the dispute "pile on" when decision makers consider actions. The late-coming interests then insist that decision makers accommodate their interests.

Other times, brinksmanship is attempted but then perceived as "crying wolf" when the crisis never materializes. Then advocates trying to bring the issue to the brink lose trust and credibility with decision makers and power brokers.

For more than a century, both development and environmental advocates have used brinksmanship strategies to build legitimacy and credibility and to bring about a crisis. The objective is to trigger Congressional action or to galvanize public support for controversial proposals.

For example, the timber industry has long supported brinksmanship aimed at delivering wood products to mills and consumers. This approach began in the 19th century with the declaration of a possible "timber famine," which led to the creation of the federal Forest Reserves. More recently, development and community interests have supported timber harvest and fire fuels reductions intended to prevent falling into the abyss of large-scale, catastrophic wildfires.

During environmentalism's Second Wave, advocates used perceived threats to fish, wildlife, open space, and scarce natural resources and conditions to drive public support for extensive environmental legislation. Later, they justified litigation to enforce those laws with the same "edge of the abyss" arguments. These advocacies were often effective if advocates based them, at least partially, on facts and presented arguments that "resonated" with politicians and their citizen supporters.

Recognizing and Dealing with Dirty Tricks

In *Getting to Yes,*[24] authors Roger Fisher and William Ury divide dirty tricks into three categories: *"deliberate deception, psychological warfare, and positional pressure tactics."* They recommend that you be prepared to deal with all three kinds. I do too.

To summarize their list of "deliberate deceptions," they say that these include "phony facts," "ambiguous authority," and "dubious intentions." They point out that disputants

---

[24] *Getting to Yes: Negotiating Agreement Without Giving In.,* Fisher, Roger and Ury, William. Penguin Books USA, Inc. NY, NY. 1981. pp.132-142.

are not required to disclose all facts or bargaining positions, so nondisclosure is not in and of itself deception. Lately, the media has covered the use of "**pretexting**" which is deliberate fakery or misinformation designed to obtain information, confuse a disputant, or cause disputants to misstep. In other cases, you might hear the term "**managing perceptions**" which, similar to pretexting, is the use of limited or deceptive messages to manipulate opinion and achieve outcome control. Pretexting and managing perceptions fit in the "deliberate deceptions" category.

"Psychological warfare" includes creating "**stressful situations**," conducting "**personal attacks**," presenting a "**good guy/bad guy routine**," and issuing "**threats**." The category "positional pressure tactics" contains "**refusal to negotiate**," "**escalating demands**," having a "**hard-hearted partner**," asking for "**a calculated delay**," or stating "**take it or leave i**t."

I suggest you get a copy of *Getting to Yes* to read more about their list of dirty tricks as well as their entire interest-based bargaining method.

In addition to Fisher and Ury, I suggest readers look at the writings and ideas of Saul Alinsky. In the late 1960s and early 1970s, he published books and articles about techniques for disrupting processes, heightening disputes, and radicalizing politics. Today, people use many of his techniques as power plays, pressure tactics, and non-EDR means to precipitate crisis.

In 2007, the Federal Emergency Management Agency (FEMA), an agency within the Department of Homeland Security, held **a mock press conference** in which agency leaders were questioned by agency personnel masquerading as reporters. This is a normal practice called "**a murder panel**" or "**mock media**" **event**. The difference was that FEMA called it a press conference and invited the actual media to participate by phone, without permitting the working press to ask questions. Instead, the actual media people listened to a series of "softball" questions posed by FEMA employees to their bosses. Although FEMA got its messages out, their dirty trick lost FEMA credibility with the media and the resulting mistrust was destructive to FEMA's interests.

Applying Techniques at Different Geographic Scales

When considering scale in EDR work, leaders should be looking for combinations of techniques with scale-appropriate characteristics (e.g., a referendum is not possible nationally because no authority exists to empower it but it is possible at state and local levels where local authority permits). Usually, a mixture of techniques, some narrowly and other broadly focused and some short-term and others long-term, will provide a more robust and effective program. Leaders should also be looking for community- and individual-appropriate techniques aimed at reaching communities and people that must be a part of a successful EDR effort.

As shown in the next two figures, you will readily see that dispute stage and geographic scale matter in building and implementing an EDR program. The methods for working with a dispute-resolution community of ten people engaged on a single issue are quite different from those for working with a sports-stadium full of people, or indeed with the whole nation on a looming global environmental crisis. The organization, communications, processes, techniques, activities, and timelines will necessarily vary significantly, even if the goals, objectives, and core concepts do not.

For example, when group size in a meeting exceeds five or six people, many participants experience "fright: flee or fight, hunker-down, submit, appease/placate, or deceive" feelings. If EDR leaders choose meetings as a technique and expect people to participate effectively, then the leaders must employ some means to promote calm and thoughtful participation, such as limiting group size and having facilitators for each group.

This approach will work well for groups of ten to 100 participants. If leaders address logistical difficulties, it will work for a dispute-resolution community that fills a pro football stadium. It will not work for engaging a whole river basin with millions of people in it, let alone for a state or a nation.

Generally, **the greater the geographic scale, the more techniques will cost in people's effort, money, and time.**

Ecological Scale and Some EDR Technique Choices (adapted from the National Hierarchical Framework of Ecological Units shown in <u>Theory and Principles</u> Chapter 4 and Appendix A)

Ecological unit	General polygon size	EDR Considerations
Domain	1,000,000s of square miles	**Communities**: institutions, groups and individuals with global and national power and interest **Possible techniques**: international agreements and treaties, global media, and web-based communications and meetings to support direct action
Division	100,000s of square miles	**Communities**: institutions, groups, and individuals with multi-national, national, and state power and interest **Possible techniques**: international agreements and treaties, legislation, national media, web-based communications to support direct action, and national-scale blue-ribbon committees, conferences, and working meetings
Province	10,000s of square miles	**Communities**: institutions, groups, and individuals with national and state power and interest **Possible techniques**: national and state legislation; national and regional media; web-based communications to support direct action; national- or regional-scale blue-ribbon committees, conferences, and working meetings; and collaboration/arbitration/mediation/facilitation
Section	1,000s of square miles	**Communities**: institutions, groups, and individuals with national, state, and regional power and interest **Possible techniques**: state legislation, initiatives, and referenda; national and regional media; web-based communications to provide information and support direct action; national- or regional-scale blue-ribbon committees, conferences, and working meetings; and collaboration/arbitration/mediation/facilitation methods
Subsection	10s to low 1,000s of square miles	**Communities**: institutions, groups, and individuals with state, regional, and local power and interest **Possible techniques**: state and local legislation, referenda or initiatives; national, regional, and local media; web-based communications to support provide information and support direct action; regional- or local-scale blue-ribbon committees, conferences, and working meetings; and collaboration/arbitration/mediation/facilitation methods
Landtype association	1,000s to 10,000s of acres	**Communities**: institutions, groups, and individuals with regional and local power and interest **Possible techniques**: state and local legislation, referenda or initiatives; regional, and local media; web-based communications to support provide information and support direct action; regional- or local-scale blue-ribbon committees, conferences, and working meetings; and collaboration/arbitration/ mediation/facilitation methods
Landtype	100s to 1,000s of acres	**Communities**: institutions, groups, and individuals with regional and local power and interest **Possible techniques**: state and local legislation, referenda or initiatives; local media; web-based communications to support provide information and support direct action; local-scale blue-ribbon committees, conferences, and working meetings; and collaboration/arbitration/ mediation/facilitation methods
Landtype phase	<100 acres	**Communities**: institutions, groups, and individuals with local power and interest **Possible techniques**: local legislation, referenda or initiatives; local media; web-based communications to support provide information and support direct action; local-scale blue-ribbon committees, conferences, and working meetings; and collaboration/arbitration/ mediation/facilitation methods

EDR Techniques Displayed by People, Money, and Time Costs

This figure roughly displays techniques and their related people-effort, money, and time costs. Least-cost techniques are shown around the center and costs rise towards the four corners.

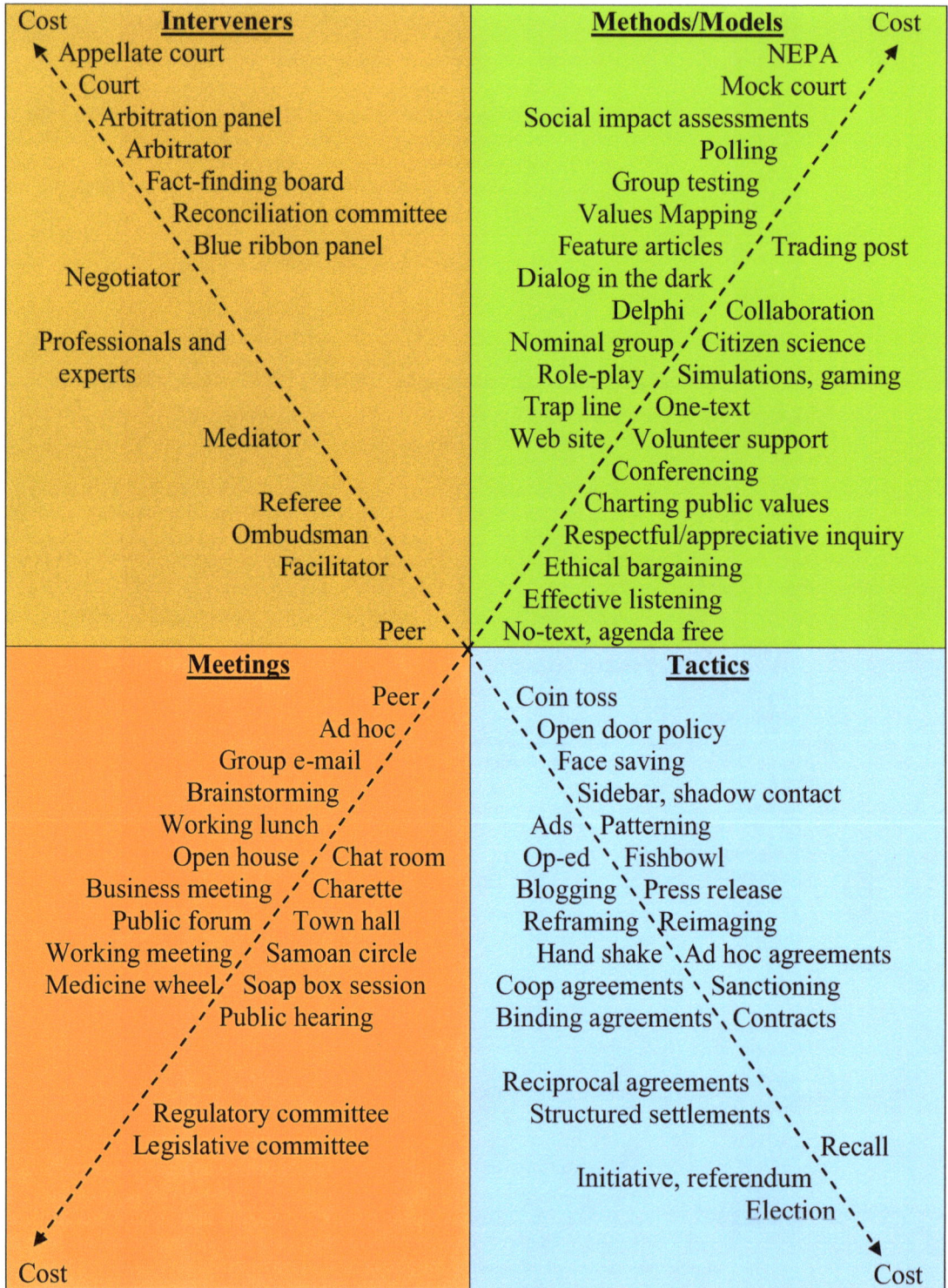

Cost **Interveners**	**Methods/Models** Cost
Appellate court	NEPA
Court	Mock court
Arbitration panel	Social impact assessments
Arbitrator	Polling
Fact-finding board	Group testing
Reconciliation committee	Values Mapping
Blue ribbon panel	Feature articles / Trading post
Negotiator	Dialog in the dark
	Delphi / Collaboration
Professionals and experts	Nominal group / Citizen science
	Role-play / Simulations, gaming
	Trap line / One-text
Mediator	Web site / Volunteer support
	Conferencing
Referee	Charting public values
Ombudsman	Respectful/appreciative inquiry
Facilitator	Ethical bargaining
	Effective listening
Peer	No-text, agenda free

Meetings	**Tactics**
Peer	Coin toss
Ad hoc	Open door policy
Group e-mail	Face saving
Brainstorming	Sidebar, shadow contact
Working lunch	Ads \ Patterning
Open house / Chat room	Op-ed \ Fishbowl
Business meeting / Charette	Blogging \ Press release
Public forum / Town hall	Reframing \ Reimaging
Working meeting / Samoan circle	Hand shake \ Ad hoc agreements
Medicine wheel / Soap box session	Coop agreements \ Sanctioning
Public hearing	Binding agreements \ Contracts
Regulatory committee	Reciprocal agreements
Legislative committee	Structured settlements
	Recall
	Initiative, referendum
	Election
Cost	Cost

EDR Technique Selection

You should always be looking for the techniques that **best fit the EDR community's situation and objectives**. For example, following a formal *negotiation* method may only have value if, during the *performing* stage, the community has identified a need to develop specific written agreements that they've otherwise struggled to form. If the community is in the *norming* stage and has a need to create a sense of shared vision and future cooperation, negotiation would be *a poor choice*.

You should also be looking for **techniques that accomplish multiple objectives**, if possible. For example, if staged and facilitated properly, a *soap box session* allows several objectives to be met simultaneously: developing shared history, expressing values, creating one-to-one communications, and practicing effective listening.

If selecting a *set of techniques*, practitioners will want to make sure the **techniques compliment one another**. For example, *interest-based bargaining, effective listening,* and *re-imaging* all work well together. Interest-based bargaining addresses how people can engage in low-conflict, values-based negotiation. Effective listening allows interest-based bargaining participants to respectfully authenticate one another's values. And practitioners can *easily bridge* from interest-based, effective-listening connection among EDR community members to *re-imaging* exercises because the skills, understandings, and behaviors of first effort compliment the next.

Finally, practitioners should recognize that **technique selection must remain low-cost to participants, flexible, and evolve** throughout the EDR effort. What works at one point in the Tuchman stages might not work later. Or, more importantly, at the point your EDR work becomes more influential and resisted, the techniques you are using may have change to meet the new challenges.

Table 1 follows and displays **four techniques categories: intervener, meetings, tactics/devices, and other methods**. The techniques categories are rated based on their **ability to support transformative or change processes: context, structure, issue, actor, and personal or group**. *Theory* Chapter 7, pages 100-101, discusses how dispute-resolution always means transformation in some respects, so Table 1 graphically displays the degree to which each technique might contribute to the five change processes.

To use Table 1, take a *look at the objectives* you set out in your EDR plan. Match your objectives to a *transformative process*. Look down the process column until you locate *one or more techniques* that seem to best support that transformative process. Initially, select *at least one technique from each of the four categories*, review the prior discussion on technique selection, and then refine your list. **Present the list to the EDR community and get their support**.

Table 1: Techniques and Their Dispute-Transforming Abilities

Transformative Processes

Intervener Techniques	Context *Ability to change context*	Structure *Ability to balance powers*	Issue *Ability to change positions, etc.*	Actor *Ability to change players/belief*	Personal/Group *Ability to change values based on education/experience*
	Very little	Some	Moderate	Very little	Very little
Peer					
Facilitator					
Ombudsman					
Referee					
Mediator					
Experts					
Negotiator			Great		
Blue-ribbon group					
Reconciliation group					Moderate
Fact-finding group					
Arbitrator					
Arbitration panel					
Local court					
Appellate court	Some	Great	Some	Some	Some

Meeting Techniques	*Ability to change context*	*Ability to balance powers*	*Ability to change positions, etc.*	*Ability to change players/belief*	*Ability to change values based on education/experience*
	Some	Some	Some	Very little	Very little
Peer-to-peer					
Ad hoc group					
Group e-mail					
Brainstorming					
Working					
Chat room					
Open house					
Nominal grp.					
Charette					
Business					
Town hall					
Forum					
Working					
Public hearing					
Regulatory committee		Great			
Legislative committee					
Soap box session					
Samoan circle					
Medicine wheel	Great	Moderate	Moderate	Some	Great

116

Tactics/ Devices	Transformative Processes				
	Context	**Structure**	**Issue**	**Actor**	**Personal/Group**
	Ability to change context	*Ability to balance powers*	*Ability to change positions, etc.*	*Ability to change players/belief*	*Ability to change values based on education/experience*
Coin toss	Very little	Very little	Very little	Very little	Very little
Open door					
Face saving					
Side bars					
Patterning					
Advertising					
Op-ed writing					
Blogging					
Fishbowl					Great
Fact-finding					
Agreements					
Ad hoc					
Hand shake					
Cooperative					
Reciprocal					
Binding					
Contracts		Great	Great		
Structured					
Elections					
Scheduled					
Recall					
Initiative					
Reframing					
Reimaging	Great	Moderate	Great	Great	Great

You're probably asking yourself if there are more things to consider in making technique selection than to what degree the techniques support the five transformative processes. You should consider these things, too:

- **Scale.** Some techniques work well locally, such as face-to-face meetings, but increasingly less well as scale increases and the numbers of people involved rises
- **Dispute stage.** Some techniques work well with disputes based on a single or a few issues between few people, such as peer mediation. For full-blown conflicts headed toward crisis, peer mediation would not work…a professional mediation team might be required. And you might want your recovery-stage techniques to be the kind to help prevent dispute recycling
- **Dispute pathway.** Most techniques will support distress work in some fashion. For scandal, techniques useful for blame de-escalation work better than, say, writing an op-ed piece. For anarchy, a coin-toss would be a bad idea because no one would commit to a new social order in such a whimsical way. In a catastrophe, conducting a mock court to "try" a hurricane would be futile and ridiculous

Other Methods	Transformative Processes				
	Context *Ability to change context*	**Structure** *Ability to balance powers*	**Issue** *Ability to change positions, etc.*	**Actor** *Ability to change players/belief*	**Personal/Group** *Ability to change values based on education/experience*
No-text, no-agenda	Some	Some	Moderate	Some	Some
Effective listening					
Ethical bargaining					
Appreciative inquiry					
Charting values					
Conferencing					
Volunteer support					
Web site					
One-text					
Trap line					
Role play				Moderate	
Simulation/ gaming					Great
Citizen science					
Delphi					
Collaboration					
Dialog in the dark					
Feature articles					
Trading post					
Mapping values					
Group testing					
Polling					
Social impact assessments					
Mock court					
NEPA/environmental analysis	Some	Some	Moderate	Moderate	Some

But perhaps the most vexing technique-selection challenge is to make sure your EDR community has the necessary money, experience, skills, and materials to pull off the technique. Some techniques require sophisticated knowledge that may have to be paid for, such as the use of professional mediators or ecologists. Other techniques require vehicles, such as aircraft, or advanced technologies, such as geographic information systems. And, although it's valuable for the EDR community to "stretch" and make use of costly, productive techniques at times, that choice must be made with consideration for all the other costs, materials, and skills implied in your EDR program plan.

Techniques in Focus

Practitioners can become enamored of, and advocates for, a particular technique. Alternatively, they can become absorbed in simply displaying their command of techniques and tradecraft. However, if practitioners cannot link techniques effectively to goals and objectives, thereby choosing the best techniques to serve the needs of a dispute-resolution community, they cannot achieve high levels of performance and effectiveness.

Having the experience and skill to find the best match between technique and outcome is **the best expression of professionalism—one that results in the least-cost, highest-satisfaction outcomes for disputants, caring onlookers, and the rest of the dispute-resolution community**.

Use of the Next Four Chapters

Readers who have a sense of what stage of dispute they are dealing with, and want to get a deeper sense of how a prescription might develop, can skip ahead at this point to any of the next four Chapters:

- ✓ Chapter 9:   Issues Abatement
- ✓ Chapter 10:   Full-Blown Conflict Resolution
- ✓ Chapter 11:   Crisis Control
- ✓ Chapter 12:   Recovery Management

Readers who wish to explore all of the material in these chapters will find that each is organized like the others with description and examples. The reader can take them in order or compare them "side-by-side," section by section.

Once they read the chapter(s), readers wishing to document elements of their own "first approximation" prescriptions can use the worksheets in Appendix B, pages 185-190.

Chapter 9: Issues Abatement

This chapter helps EDR practitioners design and implement issues-abatement programs or all four EDR pathways. If practitioners and disputants can handle disputes effectively at the issues stage, costs often remain low and satisfaction remains high.

Consult Community	Diagnose Disputes	Build Prescription	Act	Prevent New Disputes	Monitor and Adjust	Let Go or Re-consult

The difficulty with work at this stage is that the values-preference conflicts can go unresolved only to return in yet another power struggle in the near future. This is because the values disagreement still exists and practitioners and disputants involved in the low-energy, low-cost issues abatement efforts do not necessarily follow through to resolution. If disputants and participants accept such "dispute recycling", then issues abatement efforts will similarly recycle.

During the issues-abatement stage, EDR practitioners should remind disputants and participants of the unacceptable consequences of allowing dispute escalation to lead to full-blown conflict, including much higher costs, possible lower satisfaction, and delays that could injure people's values and lead to natural- and human-resource losses. If participants want dispute resolution, EDR practitioners should also be sure that the work is completed and monitored for long-term success if possible in order to avoid dispute recycling and recidivism.

Goals and Objectives

The goal for issues abatement is to bring about dispute resolution, and thereby, environmental peace and justice. See Chapter 7 for more discussion.

Objectives are set to meet the goal; they help describe the changed state that would resolve the dispute. They provide the basis for future success monitoring.

Setting objectives for dealing with disputes at the issues stage means looking at the structure, composition, and relationship factors and determining a desired status change, if any, for each factor. The desired status is expressed as an objective.

Once practitioners have a working agreement on objectives, they select techniques that are likely to attain the objectives. Practitioners and disputants then implement the techniques and monitor them for effectiveness and performance success.

Distress

A diagnosis of distress at the issues stage is based on the understanding that there are few issues, few disputants or other participants, and the dispute involves an interpersonal values difference. There may be some overtones of scandal or anarchy, but the dispute seems characterized primarily by a power struggle in which one person tries to gain ascendancy for their values over values held by others.

As practitioners examine the distress issues' structure, composition, and relationships, they can set objectives that, if attained, would indicate issue abatement success. For example, if the distress comes from a disagreement about the meaning of a law or regulation, an objective might be set to:

> "Gain full agreement on the meaning of the law or regulation"

If the dispute were compositional about the means and quality of communications around the dispute, the objective might be to:

> "Gain agreement on how each party can be effectively heard"

If the dispute were relational and about the content of the communications, the objective might be to:

> "Get communications content focused on mutual understanding and dispute resolution"

At the issues-abatement stage, practitioners should always set EDR objectives with the active participation of the disputants, and often with additional suggestions and support from other participants. EDR practitioners then look at choosing techniques that are most likely to be effective in EDR

In choosing techniques to achieve the objectives, practitioners should review the best-for-issues-abatement techniques list at the end of this chapter. The list should help practitioners to select at least two techniques to deal with each objective. For example, if the objective is:

> "Gain agreement on the meaning of the law or regulation," then two useful techniques might be:
>
> > Hold a **brown-bag luncheon** with a speaker who understands the law or regulation and have **a facilitated discussion** about understanding and values afterward; and
> >
> > Hold a series of **facilitated teleconferences** to achieve agreement on the meaning of the law or regulation, bringing in **subject-matter experts** as needed and then **documenting the agreement** when the time is right.

In the case of the selected techniques, practitioners make sure disputants are invited and confirmed for attendance, that experts, facilitators, and recorders are engaged, and that other participants critical to implementation are involved as well.

Scandal

A diagnosis of scandal at the issues stage is based on the understanding that there are few issues, few disputants or other participants, and the dispute involves an interpersonal values difference. There may be some overtones of distress or anarchy, but the dispute seems characterized primarily by a power struggle in which one person or group is claiming that their disputant has violated a law, ethic or public standard and that they should repent and change their behavior.

As practitioners examine the scandal issues' structure, composition, and relationships, they can set objectives that, if attained, would indicate issue abatement success. For example, if the scandal issue comes from a disagreement about the application of a law, regulation, moral, or ethic, an objective might be set to:

> "Gain agreement on if and how the law, regulation, moral or ethic applies to this situation"

If the dispute were compositional about the personal morality disputants held around the dispute, the objective might be to:

> "Get each disputant to understand the morals and values that the other disputants hold around the dispute"

If the dispute were relational and about the content of the communications, the objective might be to:

> "Get communications content focused on a blameless dialog about real thoughts and feelings disputants hold"

In choosing techniques to achieve the objectives, practitioners should review the techniques list to develop at least two techniques to deal with each objective. For example, if the objective is:

> "Get communications content focused on a blameless dialog about real thoughts and feelings disputants hold," then two useful techniques might be:
>
> **Train disputants on "effective listening"** and provide them with a **communications coach to assist them** as they develop their listening skills; and
>
> **Develop a "care fabric"** for each disputant (and, if wanted, for other participants) that documents their values concerning the dispute and communicates them to the other participants.

In the case of the selected techniques, practitioners make sure the disputants are invited and confirmed for attendance, that experts, trainers, coaches, and recorders are engaged, and that other participants critical to implementation are involved as well.

Anarchy

A diagnosis of anarchy at the issues stage is based on the understanding that there are few issues, few disputants or other participants, and the dispute involves an interpersonal values difference. There may be some overtones of distress or scandal, but the dispute seems characterized primarily by a power struggle in which one person or group is claiming that their disputant represents social, economic, or relationship conditions that have to change to enable a new order.

As practitioners examine the anarchy issues' structure, composition, and relationships, they can set objectives that, if attained, would indicate issue abatement success. For example, if the anarchy issue comes from a disagreement about the impact or effects of a law, regulation, moral, or ethic, an objective might be set to:

> "Gain agreement on if and how the law, regulation, moral or ethic impacts or effects minority interests"

If the dispute were compositional about whether an disputant felt unfairly or inappropriately affected by the matter in dispute, the objective might be to:

> "Get each disputant to understand the impacts of the current situation on all parties to the dispute"

If the dispute were relational and about the neglect of a minority party by people in power, the objective might be to:

> "Get conditions experienced by the minority party clearly articulated and communicated to, and then acknowledged by, the majority"

In choosing techniques to achieve the objectives, practitioners should review the techniques list to develop at least two techniques to deal with each objective. For example, if the objective is:

> "Get each disputant to understand the impacts of the current situation on all parties to the dispute," then two useful techniques might be:
>
> **Create and document direct and indirect effects** of the current situation on all parties to the dispute and **ask each disputant to prioritize their list by importance**; and
>
> Bring disputants together and **use a nominal group exercise** to set group priorities followed by a **working meeting** to address the priorities and agree on changes.

In the case of the selected techniques, practitioners make sure lists are developed and prioritized; that the disputants are invited and confirmed for attendance at the nominal group exercise; that experts, trainers, coaches, and recorders are engaged for the exercise and working meeting; and that other participants critical to implementation are involved as well.

Catastrophe

A diagnosis of catastrophe at the issues stage is based on the understanding that there are few issues, few disputants or other participants, and the dispute involves an interpersonal values difference, usually concerning the potential for, and likelihood of, a natural event leading to loss. There may be some overtones of distress, scandal, or anarchy, but the dispute seems characterized primarily by a power struggle in which one person or group is concerned about predicted negative natural or human-infrastructure incidents and desires that resources be focused on preventive actions — actions opposed by other individuals or groups..

As practitioners examine the catastrophe issue's structure, composition, and relationships, they can set objectives that, if attained, would indicate issue-abatement success. For example, if the catastrophe issue comes from a disagreement about the risk a certain natural event (such as high winds) poses to infrastructure (such as power lines and structures), an objective might be set to:

> "Gain full understanding of wind models, assumptions about effects on fixed objects, and power-line conditions and behavior during wind events"

If the dispute was compositional and about whether a disputant felt the modeling assumptions were appropriate or not, the objective might be to:

> "Get each disputant to articulate changes in assumptions they desire and then re-run the model with the new assumptions"

If the dispute were relational and about the rejection of one disputant's proposed modeling assumptions, the objective might be to:

> "Get modelers to acknowledge and incorporate the assumptions of all participants and build trust by impartial analysis and sharing of results"

In choosing techniques to achieve the objectives, practitioners should review the techniques list to develop at least two techniques to deal with each objective. For example, if the objective is:

> "Get modelers to acknowledge and incorporate the assumptions of all participants and build trust by impartial analysis and sharing of results," then two useful techniques might be:

- **Hold a brainstorming session** with the disputants and modelers to **articulate the key assumptions to be tested**; and

- Have modelers **conduct their analysis in a "fishbowl,"** with disputants and participants "looking over their shoulders" and all results shared at both draft and final stages

In the case of the selected techniques, practitioners make sure that the disputants are invited and confirmed for attendance at the brainstorming session. Then, practitioners should make sure the session is facilitated so that the key assumptions to be tested are placed on a list, that modelers are trained in fishbowl behavior and practice it, and that other participants critical to implementation are involved as well.

Implementation Considerations Common to each Pathway at the Issues Stage

Once the EDR practitioners select the techniques and refine them into an action plan with a schedule, practitioners contact disputants and other participants and otherwise prepare to support implementation.

After taking recovery actions, EDR practitioners should set a schedule for checking back with the disputants to determine if implementation has gone smoothly. They might set a 3-, 6-, and 12-month follow-up schedule to serve as their monitoring cycle and engage the mediator or negotiator periodically depending on what they find when they contact participants.

Techniques for Consideration in Issues Abatement

The table below illustrates some EDR techniques and other considerations that might be appropriate for issues abatement efforts along the four pathways. EDR Practitioners and Leaders should view the table's contents as a starting place for discussion as they consider diagnosis results and select the actual techniques most likely to meet objectives and resolve the dispute.

Readers wishing to document elements of their "first approximation" prescriptions can use the worksheets in Appendix B, pages 185 -190.

Technique Pathway	Meetings	Third Parties	Communications	Other
Distress	No-text No agenda Informal styles	Peer Mediator Mediator Counselor (MH or PTSD) Caring On-lookers	Low-key/unwritten No media Explore values Express interests/request changes if any Written agreement	Training on Effective-Listening and Interest-Based Bargaining
Scandal	One-text Informal styles	Peer Mediator Mediator Counselor/pastor Reconciliation expert/team	Low-key No media Fact checking Express interests Written agreement/changed behaviors	Training on Working/Living with Difficult People
Anarchy	One-text Informal or formal styles	Mediator Peer Mediator Negotiator	Low-key No media Express values Express interests Written agreement/changed process or rules	Training on Effective-Listening and Interest-Based Bargaining
Catastrophe	No text Informal/formal meetings	Incident leaders/mangers Counselor (MH or PTSD) Caring On-lookers	Written and unwritten Media Express interests/request changes if any	Support services (e.g., housing, food, medicines, respite care)

Chapter 10: Full-Blown Conflict Resolution

This chapter builds on the issues-abatement information from Chapter 9. This chapter concerns EDR work in the much more complicated environment of full-blown conflicts. If practitioners and disputants can handle disputes effectively at the full-blown conflict stage, they may avoid crisis and contain costs for most involved parties, at least to some degree.

Consult Community	Diagnose Disputes	Build Prescription	Act	Prevent New Disputes	Monitor and Adjust	Let Go or Re-consult

The difficulty with work at this stage is that it is often characterized by disputants with strong and fixed positions. Frequently, one disputant or another is tempted to create, or at least to allow, a rapid accumulation of events and communications to trigger a crisis that they believe will be favorable to their values, a so-called "brinksmanship" approach.

Compared to issues abatement, EDR work with full-blown conflict is high cost and high intensity; it may also be long duration. If practitioners do not achieve resolution, the potential for future escalation is often high whereupon costs can go much higher. In contrast to some shorter-term, low intensity issues-abatement efforts, the advantage of a long-duration effort is that, if practitioners build the process carefully, enough time and energy may be available to resolve disputes short of crisis.

During full-blown conflict, practitioners should remind disputants and participants of the likely unacceptable consequences of crisis, including the loss of control over events and outcomes. If participants want resolution and are willing to work for it, EDR practitioners should insure that the work is complete and monitored for long-term success, if possible, to avoid dispute recycling and recidivism

Goals and Objectives

The goal for work on full-blown conflicts is to bring about dispute resolution, and thereby, environmental peace and justice. Objectives are set to meet the goal; they help describe the changed state that would resolve the dispute. They provide the basis for future success monitoring.

Setting objectives for dealing with disputes at the full-blown conflict stage means "teasing apart" the key issues that make up the full-blown conflict and then examining the structure, composition, and relationship factors associated with each one as well as those held in common. Then practitioners determine a desired status change, if any, for each issue and associated factors, and they develop objectives that reflect those desired changes.

Once practitioners have a working agreement on objectives, they select techniques that are likely to attain the objectives. Practitioners and disputants then implement the techniques and monitor them for effectiveness and performance success.

Distress

A diagnosis of distress at the full-blown conflict stage is based on the understanding that there are many issues, many disputants and other participants, and the dispute involves many values-preference scale differences and informal and formal communication channels. The full-blown conflict often attracts many onlookers, and sometimes the media.

There may be some overtones of scandal or anarchy, but the dispute seems characterized primarily by a power struggle in which the ascendancy of one person's or a group's ideas or actions over the other is the major thrust. Onlookers may be confused about the content of those ideas, the intentions of the proposed actions, and the relative importance of the differing values and points of view.

As practitioners start examining the embedded issues within the distress full-blown conflict's structure, composition, and functions or relationships, they can set objectives that, if attained, would indicate issue abatement success. For example, if the distress comes from a disagreement about the interaction among an endangered species, air quality, water quality and periodicity, noise, and light pollution, an objective might be set to:

> "Gain understanding of and agreement on the effects of air and water quality and noise and light pollution on the purple tufted madwort and the arcane bear"

If the dispute were compositional about the means of communications around the dispute, the objective might be to:

> "Gain agreement on how each party can be promptly and effectively informed about conditions and trends affecting the purple tufted madwort and the arcane bear"

If the dispute were relational, about trust and the believability of communications content, the objective might be to:

> "Build credibility and trust among participants"

At the full-blown conflict stage, practitioners should try to set EDR objectives with the active participation of the disputants, but positioning and power plays may initially be too intense to set resolution objectives. After consultation with onlookers and participants, EDR practitioners may want to develop some initial objectives, select some techniques, and begin implementation.

As tension declines, practitioners can discuss and refine the objectives with the active participation of the disputants. EDR practitioners can then adaptively rework and revise techniques that are ever more likely to be effective in EDR

In choosing techniques to achieve the objectives, practitioners should review the techniques list to develop at least two techniques to deal with each objective. For example, if the objective is:

> "Build credibility and trust among participants," then two useful techniques might be:

> Work with disputants and other participants to **develop a set of norms for future relationships**, including an agreement **for courtesy, candor, and no surprises**; and

> Engage the services of a **coach** to assist disputants with complying with the norms and have the services of a **mediator** available if compliance concerns get raised by any party.

As regards selected techniques, practitioners make sure disputants are engaged in developing the norms and commit to them (preferably in writing); that coach, mediator, facilitators, and recorders are engaged; and that other participants critical to implementation are involved as well.

Scandal

A diagnosis of scandal at the full-blown conflict stage is based on the understanding that there are many issues, many disputants and other participants, and the dispute involves many values-preference scale differences, and informal and formal communication channels. The full-blown conflict often attracts many onlookers and the media.

There may be some overtones of distress or anarchy, but the dispute seems characterized primarily by a power struggle in which one person or group is claiming that their disputant has violated a law, ethic or public behavioral standard — and they should become compliant or receive punishment. Onlookers and the media may be confused about the circumstances and the alleged scandalous actions; many will believe the old maxim, "Where there's smoke, there's fire," and some will adopt a "wait and see" attitude.

As practitioners start examining the embedded issues within the scandal full-blown conflict's structure, composition, and relationships, they can set objectives that, if attained, would indicate issue abatement success. For example, if the scandalmonger cries about a sub-division developer failing to comply with a state's environmental-protection requirements for soils, surface water, and a rare butterfly, an objective might be set to:

> "Gain agreement on the meaning of the state's regulations and how they apply to actions on the site under development"

If the dispute were compositional about the Vision and Code of Conduct the developer has established for her business, objectives might be to:

> "Get the developer to clearly articulate her vision and code of conduct in terms of the development" and

> "Describe the means for communicating those thoughts with interested people and the media, making sure people are heard

If the dispute were relational and about the content of the communications, the objective might be to:

> "Get communications content focused on a blameless dialog, addressing each issue in order of its importance to the disputants"

In choosing techniques to achieve the objectives, practitioners should review the techniques list to develop at least two techniques to deal with each objective. For example, if the objective is:

> "Get the developer to clearly articulate her vision and code of conduct in terms of the development," then two useful techniques might be:

- Assist the Developer to **prepare and deliver an oral and verbal presentation** on her vision, code of conduct, and development; and

- Facilitate a **walking caucus** of disputants and other participants to illustrate their concerns to the Developer, **facilitate** a dialog at the caucus, and **hire a mediator** to deal with remaining issues if not resolved at the caucus.

As regards selected techniques, practitioners make sure the developer gets the presentation resources and coaching she requires to be successful. In addition, practitioners should invite the disputants and confirm their attendance at the walking caucus. A coach, facilitator, mediator, and recorder may have to be engaged, and practitioners must insure that other participants critical to implementation are involved as well.

Anarchy

A diagnosis of anarchy at the full-blown conflict stage is based on the understanding that there are many issues, many disputants and other participants, and the dispute involves many values-preference scale differences and many informal and formal communication channels. The full-blown conflict often attracts many onlookers and the media, particularly if business is disrupted, violence against people or property occurs, or arrests are made to prevent such acts.

There may be some overtones of distress or scandal, but the dispute seems characterized primarily by a power struggle in which many people or groups are claiming that their disputant represents social, economic, or relationship conditions that have to change to enable a new order. Minority versus majority issues, which are characterized as "right versus wrong" debates, and appeals to higher-order social values concerning "fairness" and "equal rights" are common.

As practitioners start examining the embedded issues within the anarchy full-blown conflict's structure, composition, and relationships, they can set objectives that, if attained, would indicate conflict-resolution success. For example, if anarchists have chained themselves to trees and earth-moving equipment at the sub-division developer's site, and if anarchists are marching at the nearby State Legislature with lots of media present, an objective might be set to:

> "Gain understanding of any disparate effects of the laws, regulations, morals, or ethics on the anarchists' values as contrasted with the rest of society"

If the dispute were compositional regarding whether an disputant felt unfairly or inappropriately affected by the matter in dispute, the objective might be to:

> "Explore the full range of options to reduce or eliminate the effects of perceived environmental injustice

If the dispute were relational and about the neglect of the anarchists by people in power, the objective might be to:

> "Issue by issue, get disputants focused on building consent and consensus"

In choosing techniques to achieve the objectives, practitioners should review the techniques list to develop at least two techniques to deal with each objective. For example, if the objective is:

> "Explore the full range of options to reduce or eliminate the effects of perceived environmental injustice," then two useful techniques might be:

>> **Create and document the range of options** responsive to the key elements of the perceived injustice and **allow each disputant to rank the options according to each option's ability to satisfy their values**; and

>> **Use a mediator to initiate dialogs among the disputants** and, when agreements are struck, **codify them in a written agreement**.

As regards selected techniques, practitioners make sure option lists are developed and ranked by the disputants according to how the options address their values, that the services of a mediator and recorder are obtained, and that other participants critical to implementation are involved as well.

Catastrophe

A diagnosis of catastrophe at the full-blown conflict stage is based on the understanding that there are many issues, many disputants and other participants, and the dispute involves many values-preference scale differences, and many informal and formal communication channels. The looming catastrophe at full-blown conflict stage often attracts many onlookers and the media, particularly if businesses seem imperiled, experts are predicting people or property losses, or officials are mobilizing troops with the possibility of evacuations and imposing martial law.

There may be some overtones of anarchy or scandal, but the dispute seems characterized primarily by a likely natural event (or series of events) that threatens people and their property. People have many issues to consider in a situation wherein uncertainty can be paralyzing but inaction can lead to significant, unacceptable losses.

As practitioners start examining the embedded issues within the catastrophe full-blown conflict's structure, composition, and relationships, they can set objectives that, if attained, would indicate conflict-resolution success. For example, if heavy rains have been falling for weeks and an earthen dam appears about to fail, officials may order an evacuation of all people living in the flood plain below the dam. People will remove whatever property they can as they leave, and they will remain in shelters or with friends or family until the emergency is over or the dam fails. If the dam fails, people will raise the question of legal liability for the damage to property and loss of life. In this case, a structural objective might be set to:

> "Gain full understanding of who is liable for dam maintenance and failure and what this means for potential losses"

If the dispute was compositional and about whether an disputant felt the liable party should pay for losses they were not obviously required to assume, the objective might be to:

> "Get disputants to express their values and expectations concerning losses"

> "Explore options for satisfying the disputants' values"

If the dispute were relational and about the rejection of one disputant's settlement offer, the objective might be to:

> "Revisit options with disputants and seek values- or interest-based consensus"

In choosing techniques to achieve the objectives, practitioners should review the techniques list to develop at least two techniques to deal with each objective. For example, if the objective is:

"Revisit options with disputants and seek values- or interest-based consensus," then two useful techniques might be:

Articulate the range of options in terms disputants will understand and using presentation methods adapted to their learning styles; and

Train disputants on values- or interest-based bargaining and facilitate or mediate them to consensus.

Regarding selected techniques, practitioners make sure disputants are invited and confirmed for attendance at the values- or interest-based bargaining training session. Then, practitioners should make sure someone facilitates the bargaining session so that a consensus can emerge.

Implementation Considerations Common to each Pathway at the Conflict Stage

Once the EDR practitioners select the techniques and refine them into an action plan with a schedule, practitioners contact disputants and other participants and otherwise prepare to support implementation.

After taking recovery actions, EDR practitioners should set a schedule for checking back with the disputants to determine if implementation has gone smoothly. They might set a 3-, 6-, and 12-month follow up schedule to serve as their monitoring cycle, and engage the mediator or negotiator periodically depending on what they find when they contact participants.

Techniques for Consideration in Full-blown Conflict Resolution

The table below illustrates some EDR techniques and other considerations that might be appropriate for conflict resolution efforts along the four pathways. EDR Practitioners and Leaders should view the table's contents as a starting place for discussion as they consider diagnosis results and select the actual techniques most likely to meet objectives and resolve the dispute.

Readers wishing to document elements of their "first approximation" prescriptions can use the worksheets in Appendix B, pages 185 -190.

Technique / Pathway	Meetings	Third Parties	Communications	Other
Distress	One-text Simple agenda Formal styles	Mediator Coaches Counselor (MH or PTSD) Attorney	Unwritten/written No media Explore values Express interests/request changes if any Written agreement	Training on Effective-Listening and Interest-Based Bargaining
Scandal	One-text Formal styles	Peer Mediator Mediator Counselor/pastor Reconciliation expert/team Collaboration group	Unwritten/written Some media Expert fact checking Written agreement/changed behaviors	Training on Working/Living with Difficult People
Anarchy	One-text Informal or formal styles Safe haven	Mediator Peer Mediator Negotiator Reconciliation expert/team	Unwritten/written Some media Express values Express interests Written agreement/changed process or rules	Training on Effective-Listening and Interest-Based Bargaining
Catastrophe	One text Informal/formal meetings Safe haven Trap line	Incident leaders/mangers Counselor (MH or PTSD) Caring On-lookers	Written/unwritten Media Express interests/request changes if any	Fore-thought/forecast Support services (e.g., housing, food, medicines, respite care) Relocation

Chapter 11: Crisis Control

This chapter concerns EDR work in the much more chaotic and fast-moving crisis environment. If practitioners and disputants can handle disputes effectively at the crisis stage, they may avoid many unacceptable consequences of the crisis and manage the dispute to prevent recycling of past issues and conflicts.

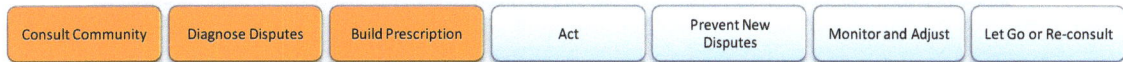

Consult Community	Diagnose Disputes	Build Prescription	Act	Prevent New Disputes	Monitor and Adjust	Let Go or Re-consult

The difficulty with work at this stage is that events and outcomes are often out of the control of the disputants and most onlookers. Events also often move quickly, adding to confusion over what is acceptable as regards outcomes. The new status quo that emerges may have many unintended results that affect both old disputants and new players in unanticipated ways.

Compared to full-blown conflict, EDR work with crisis is low cost and likely to be high intensity because it is often short duration. If practitioners do not achieve control, the potential for unacceptable and unintended losses is often high, and resulting recovery costs can be much higher. The advantage of a short-duration effort is that it permits practitioners to focus on the basic needs and wants of the disputants and other participants, while doing what they can to build dispute-resolution actions into future structures, compositional elements, and relationships. The practitioners also can begin working with the tendency to attribute blame, which can serve as a deterrent to recovery and renewal.

Goals and Objectives

The goal for work on a crisis is to address the needs and wants of disputants and other participants as they transition to a new status quo, and thereby, to promote the potential for environmental peace and justice in recovery. Objectives are set to meet the goal and help to describe the changed state that would resolve the dispute. They provide the basis for future success monitoring. Practitioners may determine a desired status change, if any, for each issue and associated factors, and they develop objectives that reflect those desired changes.

Setting objectives for dealing with disputes at the crisis stage means focusing on human needs within the context of the dispute and the crisis (see Theory and Principles page 42 for a discussion of Maslow's, Community, and Business Hierarchy of Needs). Examination of these needs, and the capabilities to assuage them, will reveal key issues that can provide focus for the crisis-control effort. As practitioners start examining the Maslow's Hierarchy of Needs issues within the crisis structure, composition, and relationships, they can set objectives that, if attained, would indicate crisis-control success.

At the crisis stage, practitioners should try to set EDR objectives with the active participation of the disputants, but time may be too short and change too intense to set control objectives with full involvement. EDR practitioners may want to quickly develop some objectives, select some techniques, and begin implementation — all while trying to keep disputants and other participants up to speed as much as possible.

As crisis peaks and moves towards recovery, practitioners can discuss and refine the objectives with the active participation of disputants. EDR practitioners can then rework and revise techniques that are ever more likely to be effective in EDR

During a crisis, practitioners should be looking forward to recovery as much as possible, helping disputants and other participants focus there too. Using forethought techniques, practitioners may find key future dispute-resolution elements by examining causal structural, compositional, and relationship factors associated with the earlier full-blown conflict and the early crisis.

Once practitioners have a working agreement on objectives, they select techniques that are likely to attain the objectives. Practitioners and disputants then implement the techniques and monitor them for effectiveness and performance success.

Distress

This crisis form may attract many onlookers, and sometimes the media if it involves public personalities or violence.

There may be some overtones of scandal or anarchy, but the dispute has grown into a distress crisis in which events and outcomes are likely to be out of the disputants' control. For example, a divorcing couple wishing to resolve a home-ownership issue may have little control over what outcome a judge or a natural disturbance event may determine.

Using another example, let's consider that the distress comes from a long-standing, escalating disagreement about an ongoing property line survey that. If the property line is relocated accurately, the new alignment might destroy the comfortable, life-long occupancy of one disputant's home. In this situation, an objective might be set to:

> "Gain agreement between disputants to assure homeowner's continued occupancy regardless of the property line location"

If the dispute were compositional about the attitudes held by disputants around the dispute, the objective might be to:

> "Make sure each disputant understands values held by the other disputants concerning accurate location of the property line"

If the dispute were relational, about the completeness of communications content, the objective might be to:

"Make sure communications are complete"

In choosing techniques to achieve the objectives, practitioners should review the techniques list to develop at least two techniques to deal with each objective. For example, if the objective is:

"Gain agreement between disputants to assure homeowner's continued occupancy regardless of the property line location," then two useful techniques might be:

Work with the disputants and participants to examine **the full range of options** for the homeowner to continue to occupy and enjoy the home; and

Engage the services of a **mediator or negotiator** to help the disputants find an acceptable option and an **attorney** to draw it up.

Selecting techniques involves making sure the disputants and land-ownership experts are engaged in developing the full range of options, that a mediator or negotiator is engaged, and that other participants critical to implementation are involved as well.

Scandal

This crisis form often attracts many onlookers. If the scandal involves elected or appointed officials or other public personalities, expect the media to engage significantly.

There may be some overtones of distress or anarchy, but the dispute has grown into a scandal crisis in which events and outcomes are likely to be out of the disputants' control. For example, a public affairs officer for a government agency gets a phone call from the media asking why his boss was photographed drinking with and taking cash bribes from a lobbyist. The public affairs officer is in a scandal crisis. The communications and outcome are already out of his control. However, he may have the opportunity to influence media coverage by acquiring and quickly disseminating accurate information.

For example, if the scandal comes from the alleged bribery example, an objective might be set to:

"Clearly communicate the applicable government ethics and the need to assure allegations are dealt with fairly and within the law"

If the compositional part of the dispute concerned interpretations of the ethics as written, the objective might be to:

"Communicate how ethics requirements fit this dispute situation"

If the dispute were relational, about the relationship between the agency head and the lobbyist, the objective might be to:

> "Get the agency head and the lobbyist to explain their relationship publicly"

In choosing techniques to achieve the objectives, practitioners should review the techniques list to develop at least two techniques to deal with each objective. For example, if the objective is:

> "Communicate how ethics requirements fit this dispute situation," then two useful techniques might be:

>> Engage the services of an **ethics expert** to interpret events under existing ethics rules, and

>> Hold a **press conference or briefing** to announce the findings, whether they are good news or bad for the agency head.

In the case of the selected techniques, practitioners should make sure disputants are involved in hearing directly from the ethics expert and allowed to ask questions at appropriate times. This should take place before any press briefing.

Anarchy

This crisis form often attracts many onlookers. If the anarchy involves hostage taking, elected or appointed officials, or other public personalities, expect the media to engage significantly.

There may be some overtones of distress or scandal, but the dispute has grown into an anarchy crisis in which events and outcomes are likely to be out of disputants' control. For example, after increasing strife over timber harvests, a radical environmental group firebombs a Bureau of Land Management seedling nursery and related barns, shed, and buildings. A month later, others of the group have chained themselves to logging equipment and to concrete barricades erected at a logging site. They are providing real-time video to the media and an internet journal and blog to interested people around the world.

For example, if the anarchy comes from the ecotage example, a structural objective might be set to:

> "Clearly state and communicate the legal violations being committed and re-state the IPMP "life preserver"[25] concerning the logging event"

---

[25] Institute for Participatory Management and Planning, Monterey, CA., www.ipmp-bleiker.com

If the compositional part of the dispute concerned the application of the law, the objective might be to:

"Restore logging operations while communicating the basis for the actions"

If the dispute were relational, about the communications between the anarchists and the Bureau of Land Management, the objective might be to:

"Encourage effective listening between organization leaders"

In choosing techniques to achieve the objectives, practitioners should review the techniques list to develop at least two techniques to deal with each objective. For example, if the objective is:

"Restore logging operations while communicating the basis for the actions," then two useful techniques might be:

Promptly **arrest the demonstrators, free the hostage equipment, remove the chains and concrete barricades**, and

Hold a **press conference or briefing** to announce the actions taken.

Selecting techniques involves making sure the disputants know what has occurred and the positions held by all parties to the dispute.

Catastrophe

This crisis form often attracts many onlookers. If the catastrophe involves loss of life and extensive property damage, expect the media to engage significantly.

There may be some overtones of distress, scandal, or anarchy, but the dispute has grown into a catastrophe crisis in which events and outcomes are likely to be out of disputants' control. For example, after years of warnings and wrangling about if and how to fix a bridge with bad decking and eroding retaining walls and piers, a 15-year flood event caused an abutment to fail. The bridge span shifted off its foundations and may collapse into the river. The bridge is not safe to cross by vehicle or on foot.

Under these circumstances, two structural objectives might be set to:

"Define the ownership and maintenance responsibilities for the bridge," and

"Create safe conditions for the traveling public"

Two compositional objectives might be to:

"Determine how people previously using the bridge can continue to meet their transportation needs," and

"Open at least once communications channel to each person or family affected by the bridge closure"

A relationship objective might be to:

"Make sure each person affected by the closure has their wants and needs heard"

In choosing techniques to achieve the objectives, practitioners should review the techniques list to develop at least two techniques to deal with each objective. For example, if the objective is:

"Create safe conditions for the traveling public," then two useful techniques might be:

Promptly **close the bridge** and **place signs** strategically to assist travelers to make good choices about what detour routes to follow, and

Hold a **press conference or briefing** to get the word out.

Selecting techniques involves making sure the affected people receive prompt notification and have a chance to share ideas with the folks in charge of the closure.

Implementation Considerations Common to each Pathway at the Crisis Stage

Once the EDR practitioners select the techniques and refine them into an action plan with a schedule, practitioners contact disputants and other participants and otherwise prepare to support implementation.

After taking crisis-control actions, EDR practitioners should set a schedule for checking back with the disputants to determine if implementation has gone smoothly. They might set a 3-, 6-, and 12-month follow-up schedule to serve as their monitoring cycle and engage the mediator or negotiator periodically, depending on what they find when they contact participants.

Techniques for Consideration in Crisis Control

The table below illustrates some EDR techniques and other considerations that might be appropriate for crisis control efforts along the four pathways. EDR Practitioners and Leaders should view the table's contents as a starting place for discussion as they consider diagnosis results and select the actual techniques most likely to meet objectives and resolve the dispute.

Readers wishing to document elements of their "first approximation" prescriptions can use the worksheets in Appendix B, pages 185 -190.

	Meetings	Third Parties	Communications	Other
Distress	One-text Full agenda Informal and formal styles	Incident staff Mediator Coaches Counselor (MH or PTSD) Attorney	Unwritten/written Some media Explore values Express interests/request changes if any	Training on Effective-Listening, Crisis Behavior, and Acceptance
Technique Pathway	One-text Full agenda Formal styles Support circle	Incident staff Mediator Reconciliation expert/team Collaboration group	Unwritten/written Press briefings Expert fact checking Rule-making	
Anarchy	One-text Full agenda Informal or formal styles Safe haven Samoan circle Trap line	Incident staff Mediator Negotiator Reconciliation expert/team Collaboration group	Unwritten/written Press conferences Rule-making	
Catastrophe	One text Full agenda Informal/formal meetings Fish bowl Safe haven Trap line	Incident leaders/mangers Counselor (MH or PTSD)	Written/unwritten Press conferences Rule-making	Support services (e.g., housing, food, medicines, respite care) Relocation

Chapter 12: Recovery Management

This chapter concerns EDR work with recovery in the aftermath of the chaos and uncertainty of crisis. If practitioners and disputants can handle disputes effectively through recovery, they may avoid many recovery issues, such as blame and priority confusion, and manage the dispute to prevent recycling of past issues and conflicts.

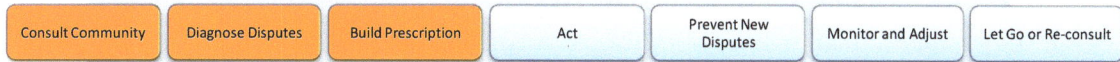

Consult Community	Diagnose Disputes	Build Prescription	Act	Prevent New Disputes	Monitor and Adjust	Let Go or Re-consult

Depending on the nature of the dispute and the crisis, recovery can take many years. Bill Bridges' book on transitions[26] is an excellent source of information about how individuals and organizations can move through what he describes as the "neutral zone" between what was before and what exists after the crisis.

Early in recovery, EDR practitioners and participants alike may be confused about what changes have occurred. The chaos and disruptions of daily life may make understanding difficult regarding how issues have been changed in substance or priority by the crisis. The emergence of blame as a communications content adds to the confusion because blame frequently targets past structural, compositional, or relationship facts and conditions so it can impede transition to full recovery.

Compared to crisis, EDR work with recovery displays variable (and sometime quite high) costs and low to moderate intensity because it is often of long duration. If practitioners do not achieve full recovery, the potential for the emergence a blame-and-victim situation and the recycling of past issues is quite high. The advantage of a long-duration effort is that it permits practitioners to focus on building dispute-resolution processes into developing structures, compositional elements, and relationships. The practitioners can also focus on blame as an issue in order to achieve blame abatement at the earliest time.

Goals and Objectives

The goal for recovery work is to address the needs and wants of disputants and other participants as they transition to a new status quo, and thereby, to promote the potential for peace and justice. Objectives are set to meet the goal and to help describe the changed state that would prevent the recycling of issues composing the dispute. They provide the basis for future success monitoring. Practitioners may determine a desired status change, if any, for each continuing and emerging issue and associated factors, and they develop objectives that reflect those desired changes.

When working with disputants and participants, EDR practitioners who are trying to set objectives for dealing with disputes at the recovery stage will find themselves returning to an issues-abatement approach against the backdrop of recent experience regarding the crisis. Generally, EDR practitioners will have structural, compositional, and relationship issues, along with key transition components of each, that were not present before the

---

[26] Managing Transitions: Making the Most of Change. Bridges, W. Da Capo Press. 2003.

crisis. With this understanding, practitioners can set objectives that, if attained, would indicate full recovery success.

At the recovery stage, practitioners should try to set EDR objectives with the active participation of the disputants, but some participants necessary for full recovery may not be immediately available. EDR practitioners may want to view objectives as evolutionary at this stage, allowing for gradual changes as participants elect to get involved. Because full recovery can take extended periods, practitioners should watch for changing participation and for shifting priorities among the objectives.

During recovery, practitioners should be looking at creating issues-abatement processes and mechanisms as much as possible, and help disputants and other participants focus there too. Using forethought techniques, practitioners may find key future dispute-resolution elements by examining causal structural, compositional, and relationship factors associated with earlier issues, conflicts, and crises.

Once practitioners have a working agreement on objectives, they select techniques that are likely to attain the objectives. While recognizing that the techniques are likely to evolve along with objectives, practitioners and disputants then implement the techniques and monitor them for effectiveness and performance success.

Distress

This recovery form may attract many onlookers, and sometimes the media if it involves public personalities or violence. As participants make progress on recovery, interest usually disappears quickly.

There may be some lingering overtones of scandal or anarchy, but the dispute has moved to a changed state, and the participants may be confused about what new conditions exist. For example, a landowner sets a prescribed fire to clear brush, and it escapes fire lines and spreads beyond prescription, burning up a neighbor's shrubbery and damaging their home. The dispute escalates quickly into a crisis right along with the fire.

In the aftermath, if the distress recovery concerns a structural legal-liability element, an objective might be set to:

> "Gain agreement between disputants on legal liability for the escaped prescribed fire"

If the dispute were compositional, about how communications agreements between disputants at the time of the prescribed fire, the objectives might be to:

> "Review communications agreements," and

> "Agree on whether agreements were kept"

If the dispute were relational, about the completeness of communications content, the objective might be to:

"Review communications content to check completeness"

In choosing techniques to achieve the objectives, practitioners should review the techniques list to develop at least two techniques to deal with each objective. For example, if the objective is:

"Gain agreement between disputants on legal liability for the escaped prescribed fire," then two useful techniques might be:

Work with the disputants and participants to select a professional **arbitrator**; and

Convene arbitration hearings and share results, if agreed to by participants, with the public.

In the case of the selected techniques, EDR practitioners may have to promote the idea of working with an arbitrator, obtain those services, and assist with convening the hearings. Other participants may have to wait for results until the arbitration, which may be closed, is complete.

Scandal

This recovery form can attract many onlookers. If the scandal is effective and involves elected or appointed officials or other public personalities, the media and the public at large may have a continuing, low-level interest during recovery. Practitioners may experience occasional "checking-in" on the "progress" of the proceedings by the media and interested people. If the scandal was ineffective, people will have little or no interest.

There may be some overtones of distress or anarchy, but the dispute has passed through a crisis and disputants can now re-exert some-to-full control. If criminal prosecution or job loss is involved, disputants may have fewer or different options than before. In those cases, recovery may involve a significant transition focus and higher levels of distress.

For example, the media exposes a minerals-industry executive for offering sexual and other favors to a state elected official. They have photos of them together in intimate settings and witness statements about their loving behavior. She vigorously defends her relationship to the female official, mentioning their plans to be together and to marry in the future. The official agrees about their relationship, mentioning that she intends to divorce her husband to establish a relationship with the executive.

The media then reveals that they took trips together, including expensive ski and golfing trips to Europe, paid for by the executive's firm; and that, after each trip, the official voted in favor of measures beneficial to the mineral industry. The media points out that this clearly violates the state's ethical standard of "no conflict of interest, not even the appearance." Public discourse also carries an undercurrent of anti-gay and anti-feminist commentary.

As the crisis is reached, the scandal becomes effective. Charged with ethics violations, the state official accepts a plea agreement and pays a fine while retaining her seat. Her husband divorces her. With the resultant notoriety, the executive decides to end the relationship. The minerals industry is reeling with the effects of the scandal and the increased media scrutiny on their business relationships. The industry informs the executive that she faces firing, and she prepares to sue. Blame erupts on all sides. The media has a field day.

Under these circumstances, structural objectives might be set to

> "Review the state's ethical requirements," and

> "Communicate how the official's agreement fits with ethics and past cases"

If the compositional part of the dispute concerns opinions about lesbian relationships, the objective might be to:

> "Gather information and communicate the realities of lesbian married couples"

If the dispute were relational, about the relationship between the executive and the minerals industry, the objective might be to:

> "Determine if the executive had appropriately communicated her relationship to her boss"

In choosing techniques to achieve the objectives, practitioners should review the techniques list to develop at least two techniques to deal with each objective. For example, if the objective is:

> "Determine if the executive had appropriately communicated her relationship to her boss," then two useful techniques might be:

>> Engage the services of a **mediator** to work between the executive and her boss to attempt a settlement and

>> Procure **post-trauma stress counseling services** for all parties.

Regarding the selected techniques, practitioners should make sure disputants feel they have been heard by the mediator. Stress counseling should be ongoing during the mediation process, but not incorporated into the mediation because of confidentiality requirements.

Anarchy

This recovery form rarely attracts onlookers, unless the anarchy was ineffective and the crisis involved hostages or loss of life. Criminal prosecution is a likely result, and under those circumstances, practitioners should expect the media to stay engaged. If the anarchy was effective, people will be interested in what changes the effective anarchy portends and will focus on related ideas and issues.

There may be some overtones of distress or scandal, but recovery primarily concerns the aftermath of anarchy — and either the rejection or acceptance of a new order. For example, a local Soil and Water Conservation District struggled for years with funding and had a hard time attracting partners. The District Board of Directors employed a large staff, even though funding had fallen steadily. As funding dried up, conservation programs had less and less impact and assistance to private landowners dwindled to almost nothing.

Private landowners felt that environmental interest groups, state health officials, and other interests were trying to make the case for reduced livestock grazing on private lands or greatly increased mitigation requirements to prevent e-coli from entering waterways. The landowners knew that the Soil and Water Conservation District was a natural partner in testing for DNA in the effluent — tests that would reveal whether the e-coli source was livestock or some other source. Unfortunately, the District Board and staff had no capability for, and little interest in, this work.

The private landowners decided to replace the District Board members in the next election with their own candidates. They did so, removed the executive director and much of the staff, formed a partnership with the Farm Bureau Federation, and tested the water. They discovered that livestock were not the source of most of the e-coli, and in this instance, anarchy was effective and successful.

With the anarchy effective, a structural objective might be set to:

> "Clearly state the legal and procedural basis for replacing board members and staff"

If the compositional part of the dispute concerned the new emphasis on the water testing, the objective might be to:

> "Clearly state the intentions for water testing and how the results will be used"

If the dispute were relational, about the communications between the new Board and old Board members and staff, the objective might be to:

> "Effectively exchange views about board actions, policies, and future focus"

In choosing techniques to achieve the objectives, practitioners should review the techniques list to develop at least two techniques to deal with each objective. For example, if the objective is:

> "Clearly state the intentions for water testing and how the results will be used," then two useful techniques might be:

>> Develop a **written statement and talking points** explaining the water-testing program, and

>> Hold a **press conference or briefing and attend interest- and place-based group meetings** to explain the program.

Selecting techniques involves stating, but not over-stating, the water-testing program and its uses clearly. To enhance recovery and build dispute-resolution capacity for the future, EDR practitioners should help the new Board and staff connect with the old Board and water-quality interests to find common ground and set the basis for future communications.

Catastrophe

This recovery form often attracts many onlookers, particularly local media and place-based interests. If the catastrophe involved loss of life and extensive property damage, expect the media to remain engaged during recovery, but most non-local people will lose interest.

There are likely to be overtones of distress, scandal, or anarchy associated with the catastrophe recovery. More than any other recovery, catastrophe is likely to display blame attribution. For example, without warning, a high-altitude tornado tears through an area designated by Congress as Wilderness and a National Park, then moves on to smash a small Rocky Mountain town. The tornado uproots and breaks thousands of trees and stacks them like jackstraws; some trees fall on horses that are in the Wilderness in an outfitter's camp, killing them. The tornado destroys homes, property, and power lines in and around the town, and the storm kills twenty people, leaving over 100 homeless.

Local people get some help from emergency responders, such as the Red Cross. As elected officials look for ways to help, the Governor makes a "disaster" declaration. People begin to question why they did not receive a warning from the National Weather Service. They begin to ask the Forest Service and Park Service if they will sell or give the trees destroyed in the storm to the local sawmills to support recovery and rebuilding. They argue that government should be more forthcoming with assistance, including temporary housing while insurance companies process claims.

As relief efforts drag on, local people and officials begin to blame government agencies and insurance companies for the delays. People are also especially bitter about their

150

perception that the Weather Service let them down. They begin to cry scandal to the press and plan a recall campaign for their local County Commissioners.

Under these circumstances, two structural objectives might be set to:

"Explain the weather service's role in predicting high-altitude tornadoes," and

"List and explain all relief programs available for tornado recovery"

Two compositional objectives might be to:

"Describe how timber can be salvaged from wilderness or park areas," and

"Open at least one communications channel to each person or family affected by the tornado"

A relationship objective might be to:

"Make sure each person affected by the tornado has their wants and needs heard"

In choosing techniques to achieve the objectives, practitioners should review the techniques list to develop at least two techniques to deal with each objective. For example, if the objective is:

"Explain the weather service's role in predicting high-altitude tornadoes," then two useful techniques might be:

Bring in **an expert on tornado prediction** from a university and have the expert investigate and report on the Weather Service's performance, and

Have the investigation and report done in **a "fishbowl" manner,** with everything open to the interested public and media.

Regarding selected techniques, practitioners should make sure that the expert has strong peer respect and support, and that the expert is willing to operate in a fishbowl manner. The practitioners will have to facilitate the fishbowl process, creating communication "windows" for place- and interest-based participants.

Implementation Considerations Common to each Pathway at the Crisis Stage

Once the EDR practitioners select the techniques and refine them into an action plan with a schedule, practitioners contact disputants and other participants and otherwise prepare to support implementation.

After taking recovery actions, EDR practitioners should set a schedule for checking back with the disputants to determine if implementation has gone smoothly. They might set a 3-, 6-, and 12-month follow-up schedule to serve as their monitoring cycle, and engage the mediator or negotiator periodically, depending on what they find when they contact participants.

Techniques for Consideration in Dispute Recovery

The table below illustrates some EDR techniques and other considerations that might be appropriate for dispute recovery efforts along the four pathways. EDR Practitioners and Leaders should view the table's contents as a starting place for discussion as they consider diagnosis results and select the actual techniques most likely to meet objectives and resolve the dispute. Readers wishing to document elements of their "first approximation" prescriptions can use the worksheets in Appendix B, pages 185 -190.

Technique / Pathway	Meetings	Third Parties	Communications	Other
Distress	No text/one-text Informal and formal Styles Fish bowl	Incident staff Mediator Peer mediator Coaches Counselor (MH or PTSD) Attorney	Unwritten/written No media Explore values Express interests/request changes if any	Training on change and transitions
Scandal	No text/one-text Informal and formal styles Fish bowl Support circle	Incident staff Mediator Reconciliation expert/team Collaboration group	Unwritten/written Some media Expert fact checking Rule-making Mailing lists/e-lists Social media	Training on change and transitions
Anarchy	No text/one-text Informal and formal styles Fish bowl Safe haven Medicine wheel Trap line	Incident staff Mediator Negotiator Arbitrator Reconciliation expert/team Collaboration group	Unwritten/written Some media Rule-making Mailing lists/e-lists Social media	Training on change and transitions
Catastrophe	No text/one text Informal/formal meetings Fish bowl Safe haven Trap line	Incident staff Counselor (MH or PTSD) Peer mediator Coaches	Written/unwritten Some media Rule-making Mailing lists/e-lists Social media	Support services (e.g., housing, food, medicines, respite care) Relocation

Chapter 13: Building and Implementing an EDR Program

This chapter gives practitioners and participants information about how to build, manage, complete, and evaluate an EDR program.

Consult Community	Diagnose Disputes	Build Prescription	Act	Prevent New Disputes	Monitor and Adjust	Let Go or Re-consult

Appendix B, pages 185 -190, provides an "EDR Program Plan Template" that gives practitioners **worksheets for eight process steps that fit within the flow diagram above**:

1. Complete dispute diagnosis (refer to worksheet on page 73, too)
2. Set priorities based on the stage and pathway matrix
3. State the EDR strategy
4. Establish EDR direction
5. Select EDR techniques
6. Set the implementation schedule
7. Engage the dispute-resolution community in implementation
8. Ensure contact and engagement of people holding power

These steps will require regular review and updates throughout the EDR program-delivery effort. Readers might want to review Appendix B before continuing.

I use the term "EDR leaders" frequently in this chapter. This term refers to appropriated and tacit power holders in the dispute-resolution community, and to EDR practitioners working to lend their skills to the EDR effort.

I organized this chapter into a dispute-resolution command section, followed by handy, sequential categories of team, small-group and dispute-resolution-community development that I adapted from Tuckman (1965).[27] I end the chapter with **a method for building, implementing, and sustaining the EDR program**, a discussion of geographic scale and techniques, and program implementation considerations.

Essentials

A successful EDR effort has some essential underpinnings:

- A committed dispute-resolution community, including leaders, practitioners, and people with the power to implement resolutions and decisions
- A clear reason for moving forward
- An EDR program plan

---

[27] Tuckman, B.W. *Developmental Sequence in Small Groups.* Psychological Bulletin, vol. 63, 1965, pp. 384-399.

- If the dispute falls within the purview of a government agency conducting decision-making, a solid public involvement plan such as the Systematic Development of the Informed Consent model offered by the Institute for Participatory Management and Planning (www.ipmp-bleiker.com)
- A well-trained EDR command and management team
- An understanding that the program work will likely follow this progression:
  - Re-establishing trust and supportive communications (relationship and function),
  - Followed by building an inclusive and effective dispute-resolution community (composition), and
  - Finally, building structural elements (laws, regulations, enforceable agreements) to ensure EDR success if the dispute-resolution community requires these elements.

Dispute-Resolution Command System

In almost every instance, dispute resolution requires that someone assume the command and management of the resolution process. "Command and management" can be low-key with a part-time or informal organization, or, depending on need, it can be high profile and include a large, formal organization.

EDR leaders who develop a well-sized and directed EDR command and management organization will gain legitimacy and credibility with the dispute-resolution community. EDR leaders can use contacts within the community as well as with experienced leaders elsewhere as a way to define organization size and composition.

I am familiar with both the military command models of the Army and Air Force, and with the Incident Command System used by emergency responders, nationwide and worldwide. I am also generally familiar with treatment-team models used by medical facilities.

I led high performing interdisciplinary teams in the development and implementation of controversial environmental programs and projects. I led high-performing leadership and management teams charged with directly investing hundreds of millions of dollars of public finances and managing billions of dollars of natural resources.

From these experiences, and my years of dealing with many hard-working people involved with environmental disputes, I suggest using a model for leading and managing dispute resolution called the "Dispute-Resolution Command System," modeled on the Incident Command System used to fight wildfires and handle other disasters such as the 9/11 attack on the World Trade Center and the massive earthquake in Haiti.

Command Staff

The purpose of a command staff is to provide leadership to the EDR effort. Leadership means to describe and enable work that meets defined goals and objectives.

According to the military maxim, command means to "Follow me." In some low-intensity cases, leadership can come from a single individual. However, in more intense and complex cases, leadership may come from several sources within the dispute community and from many available EDR practitioners.

To be effective and accountable to the dispute community, EDR leaders may choose to mimic the military model of civilian leadership over military organizations and operations, and place dispute-resolution community leaders in charge of EDR practitioners. In this case, EDR experts with experience consistent with the dispute-resolution challenge at hand report to an individual dispute-resolution leader or commission with sufficient power to implement EDR decisions and programs.

General and Specialized Staff

The Dispute-Resolution Command System divides staff into two categories: general and specialized. "General staff" refers to individuals or teams managing crosscutting organizational functions. "Specialized staff" refers to expert individuals or teams that provide narrowly focused, mission-critical resources to the EDR effort.

General staff categories can include:

1. Communications and dispute-community liaison
2. Program, strategic, and tactical planning
3. Logistics and scheduling
4. Finance and procurement
5. Information technology
6. Human resources, training, and civil rights
7. Legal
8. Law enforcement and security

Specialized staff categories can include:

1. EDR specialists and consultants
2. Facilitators
3. Critical incident stress de-briefers and counselors
4. Mental and other health professionals
5. Pollsters
6. Electronic media consultants
7. Webmasters
8. Cultural anthropologists and human ecologists
9. Legal and legislative drafting experts
10. Ecologists, biologists, foresters, botanists, and ecologists
11. Environmental management consultants and engineers
12. Community planners and planning officials
13. Land managers

14. Recreation planners and managers
15. Modelers and map makers
16. and many more

The general staff functions are common to most of my EDR operations. The level of staffing, duration and formality of the organization depends on the dispute stage. A simple, single issue might require assembling the general staff expertise for only a short time. In addition, a single individual might cover several of the general staff functions at the issue stage.

As an issue intensifies and develops into a full-blown conflict, and then to crisis and recovery, the EDR operation might well require full general staff and additional support staff for each of the general staff leaders. Work and meeting tempos might increase significantly, and people might move from occasional involvement with the EDR effort to fulltime involvement.

I would incorporate specialized staff into the command and general staff structure and operations as necessary.

Vision and Urgency

If command leadership means "follow me," causing work to be done to meet objectives, people have a right to ask "where?" and to be a part of deciding direction in most cases in our democratic society. While including the dispute-resolution community, command and general staff have to develop a strong vision for successful EDR work and demonstrate an appropriate sense of urgency for completing the effort. When combined with good, visible teamwork, command and general staff commitment, solidarity, and care for one another and the larger community speaks volumes to the dispute-resolution community — and it helps to develop momentum towards successful resolution.

The sense of shared purpose and energetic application of resources to the EDR effort has to begin with the command leaders and key supporters in the dispute-resolution community.

Teamwork and EDR Community Building

EDR success is likely to rest on effective high-performance teamwork backed by a strong EDR community, particularly at full-blown conflict, crisis, and recovery stages. Command and general staff orientation and support for team training and team behavior is critical. EDR leaders should only appoint people to command or general staff roles if the leaders know that the appointees understand teamwork and have demonstrated team performance in past EDR efforts.

EDR leaders can form teams in as many different configurations as required to complete the EDR effort. The "command and general staff" team approach can work very well for the overall program management. At the same time, EDR leaders might form a smaller "strike team" for a special assignment, such as an intensive communication effort or a facilitated "venting" session.

In addition, EDR leaders may want to separate an issue-abatement effort from longer-term work meant to prevent issue and full-blown conflict recycling. The leaders can set up a focused, short-term strike team for the issue-abatement work. While this team organizes and begins to show successful results, the leaders can charter and enable a separate team to develop the means and methods to deal with the values causing recycling.

By keeping the efforts separate, leaders can reduce the potential for confusion and apathy among dispute-resolution community members. However, leaders should also recognize that the longer-term effort requires much greater investments of energy and skill than the simpler issue-abatement work.

EDR leaders will often want to extend teamwork ideas into the dispute-resolution community because the basis for "collaboration" and other cooperative positive-sum behavior is a sense of teamwork and shared desired outcomes[28].

Tuchman Understanding and Approach

Based on B.W. Tuchman's seminal work, teams and collaborative groups will share the need to accomplish, and perhaps re-accomplish, the following steps: **framing, forming, storming, warming, norming, performing, celebrating and rewarding, adjourning, evaluating, and re-framing**.

The sequential presentation that follows does not imply that the "Tuchman" stages occur in a rigid, linear way. My experience has been that teams and groups move back and forth among these stages depending on many influences, including changing laws or court rulings, the presentation of new scientific knowledge, information or analytic conclusions, and the departure of experienced participants and appearance of new ones.

Framing

My experience is that people will avoid what appears to them to be a waste of time. If they think that what appears to be an engrained, interminable dispute is not capable of resolution, they will refuse to participate, or only engage in a token manner.

In addition, not all dispute-community members will participate initially because they feel they benefit from the dispute or the status quo. Many may not agree that resolution is necessary. Although there are exceptions, opponents with the strongest value-

---

[28]Integrations of Eugene, OR offers a strong team-building training and support program aimed at aligning team behavior with mission, vision and principles. Contact: www.integr8.com or 541.485.7708

preference differences are often the last to agree. However, for work to begin, some dispute-community members must call for "space-clearing" work to start.

Building a frame house begins with clearing a space and construction begins with pouring a foundation, which is followed by framing the walls and roof with dimension lumber. Once the lumber frame is up, builders have created an outline of and structure for what will be the finished home. In EDR work, when representatives from the dispute community recognize and agree that a dispute is leading to unnecessary and unwanted consequences, the work of "clearing the space" has occurred.

When those dispute-community representatives establish a mutual good-faith intention to resolve the dispute and recruit as many supporters for the effort as they can, they have "poured the foundation" and have established a core group around which a dispute-resolution community can form.

The core dispute-resolution community may be "do-it-yourselfers" or they may want a "contractor to build their house." In either case, they can bring in trained, experienced, and well-informed EDR practitioners to help. That "help" can be advising and coaching the dispute-resolution community in their personally managed work, or it can be full, hands-on program building, execution, and evaluation by the practitioners with dispute-community consent.

Framing means developing an initial dispute diagnosis, including the consequences that would likely occur if the effort fails. Then the framers prescribe initial dispute-resolution goals and objectives, communications, processes, techniques, activities, tasks, and timelines. Framers should strive to work publicly as much as they can – in "the fishbowl" of public scrutiny – to build confidence in, and credibility for, their efforts. When the initial effort is complete, the practitioners and representatives have framed, or outlined, the "**first approximation**" of the EDR program.

EDR framers will likely base first-approximation and later programs on changing structural, compositional, or functional and relationship elements of the dispute. They will reflect the methods and means for formulating these changes in all aspects of the program.

If EDR leaders believe that the nature or intensity of the dispute warrants transformative or scoping-skill changes, practitioners will want to emphasize appropriate education, coaching, communications, values-clarification, and other actions in program activities and tasks. As stated in Chapter 7 of <u>Theory and Principles</u>, transformative steps could include:

- Committing to EDR process and outcomes
- Creating positive imaging for self, opponents, and mutual functions and relationships
- Releasing anger and blame safely
- Dropping fears and frustrations

- Stating and pursuing wants, desires, and interests
- Creating collaboration
- Refusing to recycle disputes in favor of building community

In setting goals and objectives, the framers should identify those objectives that can serve as measures of progress or benchmarks. They should also identify objectives that can serve as measures of success for the later evaluation step that will examine assumptions, performance, and accomplishment.

Methods and means of communicating about the dispute and dispute-resolution process are important first elements. These should cover all aspects of communications, including "no-surprises," media-contact, public participation, and confidentiality agreements.

Dispute-resolution community representatives and practitioners also have to outline initial dispute-resolution processes, techniques, activities, tasks, and timelines, rolling them together to give a clear picture of the EDR effort. From this initial description, participants should be able to approximate time and financial costs and feasibilities.

Remember that someone has to pay in time and money for the EDR work. Citizens often assume that EDR is a governmental function, and it may be in the government's interest to pay for a portion or all of the work. However, most agencies do not have explicit direction to conduct EDR nor budgets to support it. In addition, as part of a power play by opponents, agencies may have their budgets cut to reduce EDR efforts if elected officials and the moneys they appropriate do not explicitly endorse them.

Therefore, one of the tasks for EDR advocates is to line up explicit budgetary support for EDR efforts from public, and perhaps private, sources. This work can begin once EDR leaders develop the first-approximation program and explicitly include potential financiers in the effort.

Forming

When framers have described the first-approximation of the EDR program, they must conduct strong outreach to the communities of interest, place, tradition, and fate – communities and individuals that have a stake in the dispute and likely must participate for the dispute-resolution community to be effective. This outreach effort should be fully transparent to all participants.

People doing the outreach share the first-approximation of the EDR program with the people contacted. They emphasize the initial nature of their efforts and underscore the importance of the effort by describing and discussing the consequences of a failed EDR effort. They explain why they framed the effort and how EDR experts have been involved. If laws or regulations support their efforts structurally, they mention that fact as well and point to all the reasons they would be acting even if there were no laws requiring the work.

After the outreach, the dispute-resolution community expands to include new recruits, many of whom may be quite fearful and skeptical. This is the **forming** stage. Some may be intentional vetoers, power brokers, or power players hoping to perpetuate or escalate the dispute. Some may be interested in sabotaging the EDR work. If the expanded dispute-resolution community convenes, framers should discuss these possibilities frankly, emphasizing why resolution is important and in everyone's interest.

The broader the representation and the greater the commitment of the expanded dispute-resolution community to EDR success, the more likely the program will be effective. To get underway, the expanded community will have to decide on their initial EDR management model, including leadership and decision-making methods. They then can begin work on the second program approximation and move into the next stage.

Storming

Blaming, criticism, venting frustrations, diminishment of others, reduction of other people's opinions and values to absurdity, and all other manner of "**storming**" will likely appear during the forming process. Storming behavior will reoccur throughout the EDR effort, usually with declining intensity and frequency as the dispute-resolution community first becomes productive and then performs better and better.

While working to guide and focus the venting, EDR practitioners and caring onlookers must openly welcome it, helping participants to understand why disputes happen, and helping them to begin to understand other participants' values. EDR workers then show the dispute-resolution community that they can refocus the storming into positive outcomes such as the creation of group norms, improved components for the second-approximation of the EDR program, and information-needs lists.

Efforts to refocus storming use the "behind every criticism or fear lies a desired condition or outcome" thinking that allows opponents to reframe their values dispute. In addition, workers also use the "let's make the pie bigger" thinking to help participants escape the "must compromise," zero-sum thinking that pervades many long-term disputes. At an appropriate time, they also begin to use humor, leading the group towards laughter to help participants relax and engage more personally with one another and the EDR effort.

Warming

After guiding the dispute-resolution community through a strong first storming effort, EDR practitioners and leaders should invite the group to get to know one another better. This may begin with an introductory icebreaker effort, with participants asked to give their name and reasons for attending in the most low-key way possible. A values-oriented discussion should follow, covering the full range of values held by the participants, from object-related to rights-related or spiritual.

I ask people to speak to their own values, not their assumptions about the values of other people. I also ask them to speak to the experiences that shaped those values for them. I take these assertions at face value and record the values presented. I ask the group to recognize the shared values that they hold and respect the ones about which they disagree. Later in this **"warming"** stage, I usually punctuate the work with numerous breaks so that people have time to visit and build community cohesion.

Practitioners and participants may call for values-based discussions and warming work repeatedly throughout the EDR effort, often after a storming event or a change in the EDR program.

Norming

EDR leaders can guide the thoughts and emotions flowing from the forming, storming, and warming stages into creating rules and norms to help guide dispute-community behavior during EDR work. These rules and norms should be explicitly stated, documented, and consented to by the participants, and they should be displayed during group meetings or functions. The rules and norms should be publicly available and revised when new understanding or unanticipated situations call for changes. Leaders should explain that the rules and norms reflect a good-faith commitment, a mutually arrived at and mutually binding agreement that is the product of the **"norming"** stage.

Rules and norms vary by dispute stage and EDR scale. Consider using some of the following sample EDR group norms to initiate a discussion within the dispute-resolution community and create a list to which all participants eventually have to consent:

> "We agree to:
> - Trust and follow the EDR program we mutually design and revise
> - Stay in the process and not exit mentally, emotionally, or physically
> - Keep all participants physically, emotionally, and mentally safe
> - Respect other people's values and experiences of life
> - Be honest, candid, and civil
> - State wants and interests clearly
> - Suspend mental and verbal judgment and criticism
> - Do not act out frustrations and fears
> - Avoid threats and coercion
> - Listen without interrupting or forming a response
> - Be ready to accurately restate the comments of others
> - Avoid side conversations during meetings and events
> - Keep time, schedule, and work commitments
> - Accept ambiguity to make progress
> - Celebrate successes"

When norms are finished, EDR leaders should guide dispute-resolution community work toward agreeing to the second-approximation of the EDR program. If the second-approximation program is inadequate, leaders may rework it into a third-approximation working program that, subject to ongoing minor revisions, participants can implement effectively.

Performing

With framing, forming, storming, warming, and norming stages accomplished at least initially, EDR leaders can press forward with **performing** the EDR program. To keep the dispute-resolution community engaged and supportive, leaders will want to perform on time, to standard, and within budget as described in the program.

EDR leaders should manage the program under "continuous-improvement" principles and methods. This involves using formal and informal critique, feedback, and program revisions and adaptations after each task and activity is completed.

During the performing stage, EDR leaders should reiterate and reemphasize goals and objectives, rules and norms, and the consequences of unsuccessful EDR — restating these things frequently and publicly. In addition, the faster the pace, the more effective and energetic the communications efforts and EDR program updates have to be.

During the performing stage, people wanting to sabotage or veto the EDR effort may appear for the first time. In fact, if they perceive that they have values, power, coalitions, or other interests at risk, they may have held out until this point and may intervene strongly and without warning. The dispute-community representatives taking the lead during the forming stage will likely have identified these folks, and EDR leaders should have reached out to them.

Intervention by potential saboteurs will test the cohesiveness and commitment of the dispute-resolution community, particularly powerful interests not always present in program activities but necessary to a successful resolution. Making sure their intervention gets "sun shined" to the dispute-resolution community and the public at large will greatly diminish the likelihood of their success. EDR leaders should have contingency plans for potential saboteurs in place before beginning the performing stage and means in place to bring them into the EDR program if possible.

Celebrating and Rewarding

As milestones and objectives in the EDR program are successfully accomplished, EDR leaders have to lead the dispute-resolution community in **celebrating and rewarding** people's efforts. To be effective, celebrations and rewards have to represent real accomplishments and reflect a careful combination and balance of community and individual recognition. The intention is to build cohesion and avoid jealousy.

Leaders also must assure that recognition is not going to be embarrassing for some participants, particularly those who want their contributions to be low-key or go unnoticed.

Depending on the nature and timing of the accomplishment, EDR leaders may want to communicate the celebration and rewards story to the public at large. I usually save broad-scale public communication until late in an EDR effort, until after the dispute-resolution community has attained tangible and important results, but I recognize that sometimes these communications are important for building public support for an EDR effort.

Adjourning

When the dispute-resolution community attains the EDR program objectives and meets their goals, the EDR effort is over. This triggers the **adjourning** stage. At this point (or just before), many participants will disappear, similar to the last ten minutes of a sporting event when fans start flocking to the parking lot and heading home.

Sometimes, EDR leaders sponsor a final celebration with steadfast participants, and then everyone moves on to other parts of their lives. A public recognition of this adjournment celebration and the end of the effort is important for both the participants and the public at large.

Other times, community cohesion is so great that participants challenge leaders to tackle new dispute challenges. For all the passion and commitment of these participants, EDR leaders should be wary of the idea that a community formed to resolve one dispute could then take on another, different dispute.

At a minimum, tackling the new dispute will require the accomplishment of a new dispute-community-based framing stage and the formation of a new dispute-resolution community. The new community may share many members with the old one, but it must also incorporate new leaders and members. In addition, EDR leaders will have to begin a completely new discussion of feasibility, and the emerging dispute-resolution community will have to repeat the forming, storming, norming, and performing stages.

Once participants understand these realities, they may still want to proceed, and leaders should not discourage that intention. Otherwise, we will not be building holistic and preventative EDR capacity into our communities.

Evaluating and Re-framing

EDR leaders, opponents, and caring onlookers should evaluate an EDR program at intervals after adjournment, and they should develop an understanding of "lessons learned" to be shared with the dispute-resolution community and the public at large. **Evaluating** and communicating about effectiveness of the EDR effort may lead to better performance by all participants in the future and serve as a model for other EDR efforts. Leaders may also use it to refine structural, compositional, or functional and relationships changes that have been put in place

Evaluation may also result in **re-framing** the dispute for further work to prevent dispute recycling. A re-framed dispute at this point is likely to require much less effort than the first program did.

Re-framing may also result in re-initiation of EDR, now newly focused on another dispute that is perhaps consistent with the desires of the dispute-resolution community members who were active in the previous EDR program.

Four Environmental Problems or Opportunity Categories

My experience indicates that only four environmental problem or opportunity categories exist. These categories allow us to organize EDR efforts aimed at problem solving or opportunity seizing quickly and simply. Of course, each dispute concerns a unique set of detailed human and environmental information, and building that detailed understanding can be very challenging. However, these basic categories give us a way to organize and to build the understanding — and to mutually share information:

Human Factors

1) Consumptive
   Renewable [plants, animals, protozoa]
   Non-renewable [minerals, gases]
2) Non-Consumptive
   Recreational
   Essence [impressionistic, intuitive, spiritual, ritual, religious uses]

Environmental Factors

3) Rare, threatened, endangered, or unique environmental conditions
   Species
   Habitats
   Phenomenon
4) Understanding, prevention, and mitigation of unwanted impacts
   Natural events
   Human uses

Using this understanding as a template or outline, EDR practitioners can ask participants to state their values and locate those values geographically when possible. When we supplement this information with discussion and information about time and geographic scale, we get a sense of what people feel is at stake in the dispute.

Practitioners can ask participants to explain what their desired future use or condition might be, establishing a basis for options for changing structural, compositional, or relationship and functional factors.

Participants will often point out that, as components of natural and human systems, these elements relate one to another. For example, Category 1, "Human Uses," has a close relationship with Category 4, "Understanding, Prevention, and Mitigation of Unwanted Impacts." Categories 1, 2, and 3 may help define some of the background for trips down Distress, Scandal, and Anarchy Pathways. Categories 3 and 4 may provide context for a trip down the Catastrophe Pathway.

Systems work reveals to us that everything connects to everything else. I sometimes draw a "bubble chart" to illustrate this point with lines and arrows connecting the use-condition or resource-condition "bubbles." I label the lines to indicate the functions or relationships that link, drive, and illustrate the complexity of the system.

Implementing the EDR Program

People work best with a sense of direction — focusing their energy towards shared goals, clear techniques and a schedule — and the ability to make positive contributions. EDR leaders will want **to create an EDR command staff, complete an initial plan, and begin implementation,** taking the team and the dispute-resolution community through the "Tuchman" stages as quickly and as comfortably for participants as possible.

As momentum builds, EDR leaders will want to consult frequently with dispute-resolution community members, particularly opponents, caring onlookers, EDR practitioners, and powerful people who have a significant role in achieving resolution and preventing recycling. Many of these people will want to know about how EDR efforts are reaching important milestones, meeting objectives and goals, and attaining measures of success important to them and their constituencies.

In the end, the dispute-resolution community, and the larger community affected by its efforts and successes, must be convinced that[29]:

- Leaders dealt with people fairly — even the most difficult, confrontational people
- Participants were consulted, listened to, and heard
- Processes used were equitable, effective, and appropriate to the challenge (neither too much or too little)
- Outcomes were tangible and beneficial, and results were measurable
- Ultimately, imperatives for peace and justice were served

---

[29] Adapted from the Bleiker "life-ring" approach. See www.ipmp-bleiker.com

Chapter 14: Preventing Dispute Reoccurrence and Recycling

Efforts to prevent dispute reoccurrence and recycling begin early in an EDR effort. Once the dispute-resolution community convenes, EDR practitioners have several considerations related to prevention and mitigation.

Consult Community	Diagnose Disputes	Build Prescription	Act	Prevent New Disputes	Monitor and Adjust	Let Go or Re-consult

Part of this work is to explicitly confront the potential for dispute reoccurrence and recycling with both the dispute-resolution community and other communities. Practitioners have the responsibility to education these folks about the potential and engage them to develop specific preventive means. And, as mentioned in Chapter 13, another part of the work may be reframing the original dispute so that it builds community rather than tearing it down.

Rumor Management and Control

Rumors can erupt in any dispute-resolution effort, particularly during early organizing work. When the dispute is traveling the scandal pathway, rumors can be unusually prevalent and difficult to manage and control.

Over time, I have developed a method to handle rumors that seems to work. At times, I have even specifically assigned staff to be on the alert for rumors so we could deal with them promptly and effectively:

- Inoculate—if an event or situation is likely to cause a rumor, get the word out early with clear, supportable rumor-control messages
- Scan – EDR leaders should be scanning their environment for rumors concerning the EDR effort including issues, staffing, perceived bias, etc.
- Detect and describe – once a rumor has been detected, EDR leaders should immediately begin to better define the rumor and promptly begin rumor management and communications
- Confront the rumor not the monger – EDR leaders should always publicly confront the rumor and not attack the rumormonger; private discussions with the monger are fine if leaders have genuine clarity about the monger's identify
- Create safety and comfort for gossips – once a rumor is out, people will repeat it and speculate about it; EDR leaders should let people know they do not condone the rumor but that people should feel free to talk; if gossips feel threatened, they can raise their concerns to a neutral party of their choice
- Communicate long-term – once rumors start, they tend to persist; so, rumor management and control should be built into any long-term communications actions taken in support of the EDR effort
- Manage, monitor, reinforce messages – once EDR leaders have begun to manage a rumor, they should monitor the control efforts and adjust and reinforce messages that confront the rumor.

I have found this approach "clears" rumors quickly. The key is inoculation and early detection through effective scans.

Engage the Dispute-Resolution Community in Removing or Mitigating Impediments to Success

This element focuses EDR work on individuals, particularly those key to dispute resolution, such as the opponents and key power holders, with the intention of working through their individual values disputes and issues sufficiently to make the EDR effort successful, and later to avoid reoccurrence and recycling. Leaders should explicitly state and attempt to resolve the perceived impediments held by the several key parties. This is a sensitive matter in many cases, so techniques considered for this work might be those involving confidentiality and one-on-one engagement. Some of the techniques chosen for impediment-removal work might go on concurrently and sometimes extend well beyond the actions taken to resolve the core community-focused dispute.

Here are some considerations for addressing each of the impediments mentioned in Chapter 6 (Coltri/Caplan):

Motivation to seek vengeance – the desire for revenge flows from a participant's sense of being powerless and unfairly or oppressively treated. If EDR leaders want to mitigate the desire for revenge, they will want to ask the revenge-seeking participants what it will take to compensate them and what will prevent further perceived unfair or oppressive treatment. The practitioners are making a direct appeal for a values-preference-scale statement from the revenge-seeking parties. EDR practitioners will likely have to negotiate any responsive actions among opponents. Careful and successful work here can form the basis for increased knowledge-based and identification-based trust.

Meta-disputes (disputes about how disputes are handled) – this impediment can concern every aspect of dispute management, including values-based concerns about fairness, staff competency and biases, timing of events and conclusions, communications, and value and efficacy of actions. EDR leaders should be open to changes as they work through the several program plan approximations associated with building the dispute-resolution community.

Mistrust – calculus-based, knowledge-based, and identification-based trust development are early and often considerations as EDR leaders build community. In the team- and community-building effort, leaders should pay close attention to trust building, particularly during the framing, forming, storming, warming, norming, performing, and celebrating and rewarding stages. EDR practitioners may have to use methods emphasizing venting, values clarification, and reconciliation, particularly in early stages.

Vastly different perceptions of reality – differing values shape people's different life experiences. EDR leaders who help people clarify their values and express them clearly through anecdote or example will find that they can build awareness, understanding, and changed interpersonal treatment and communications within the dispute-resolution community. Efforts may be iterative, depending on the degree to which practitioners can assist the community to build trust.

Over-commitment and entrapment (an opponent commits too much to reverse their position later) – EDR leaders can sometimes deal with this impediment by "making the pie bigger," putting more resources or options in front of the opponents. Because this impediment may also exist because of opponent isolation from the community at large, another option, after values-clarification, is to create a welcoming dispute-resolution community that respects the past but emphasizes resolution. Most participants want the dispute to become "unstuck." Based on how they shaped their experience, they fear that they will lose something in the process. If EDR leaders confront this fear objectively and point out that many participants share it, they can then call for people to clarify what they desire.

Lack of ripeness (opponents do not agree on the dispute's urgency) – ripeness concerns reflect an opponent's perceptions of risk and reward, or their priorities based on their values. Sometimes one opponent's assertions about ripeness reflect positioning intended to confound the perceived agenda of an opponent. EDR leaders can begin to overcome this impediment by clarifying values with participants. EDR practitioners can then create the plan for the dispute-resolution community that visibly allows the community to address and overcome all issues. This plan will allow opponents to "buy in" to the overall EDR effort.

Jackpot Syndrome (one opponent looking for a big, unrealistic payoff) – revenge or a misunderstanding of potential payoffs, monetary or as regards power, may motivate participants to seek a jackpot outcome. EDR leaders can deal with impulses towards revenge as noted earlier. Leaders can explore potential payoff issues by using experts to provide examples of similar past situations and their respective payoffs. As participants buy in to efforts to build the dispute-resolution community, practitioners will find that participant expectations for a jackpot go away or greatly diminish.

Loss aversion – participants may anticipate losses from participation or EDR outcomes. Practitioners may develop a dialogue among participants about loss perceptions and the bases for them, asking participants to describe desired outcomes. Practitioners can then incorporate the desired outcomes into the EDR program.

Linkages (to other disputes, opportunities, or opponents and partners) – participants are sometimes reluctant to commit to EDR on one dispute because it links to another, or they may perceive that resolution could influence the outcome of another dispute or power struggle. EDR leaders may want to identify those linkages and either expand the dispute-resolution effort to be inclusive (making the pie bigger) or may want to agree to a step-wise dispute resolution effort that only reaches conclusion for component issues when the whole issues set has been addressed.

Conflicts of interest (team members and powerful people) – conflicts of interest, or perceived conflicts of interest, are common in small communities and among the relatively few people and groups interested in a certain resource or environmental condition. EDR leaders should be willing to declare their interest conflicts and create an open communications environment about potential conflicts.

Excluded stakeholders (caring onlookers, other participants, powerful people) – from the forming stage of dispute-resolution community, EDR leaders have to be concerned about having the right people present in, or available to, the EDR effort. If participants perceive that the right people are not present or available, then they may perceive diminished chances for success, and they may choose to exit or not participate.

Disempowered opponent – EDR leaders may have to address power asymmetry among opponents and other participants. Power relationships must approach symmetry, particularly among the opponents and any powerful interests needed for a resolution. As a prerequisite for success, EDR leaders must be alert to the requirement for approximate power symmetry among participants. Leaders should hold candid discussions with participants early in the community-building and first-approximation of the program efforts.

Unpleasant opponent – either consciously or unconsciously, some participants will disrupt EDR efforts because of their unpleasant behavior. Such participants use interruptions, polemics, and personal attacks to attempt to express their values and determine the outcome of EDR efforts. EDR leaders must deal with such behaviors by creating group norms that focus on civility, and then they must use group dialogue to reinforce and impose the norms when violated.

Competitive culture or subculture – competition among ideas should be encouraged in EDR efforts, but as is the case with an unpleasant-opponent situation, excessive competition can disrupt EDR efforts. EDR leaders should engage directly with the individuals and groups exhibiting this behavior. Because the competitive behavior is cultural, EDR leaders should make sure to acknowledge and respect the values represented by the culture. However, they should be sure to emphasize and norm more cooperative behaviors for the dispute-resolution community.

Preoccupation with risk and uncertainty – EDR practitioners find that many environmental disputes rest on perceived risks to resources from human or natural phenomenon or on risks to human communities. Some participants may focus excessively on risk or on the uncertainties that surround effective actions. EDR leaders may have to focus on trust building and effective presentation of scientific knowledge or management experience to help mitigate this behavior. They can use stepwise, "adaptive" EDR actions to build trust and understanding about effective resolution efforts; adaptive actions refers to using each round of actions as experiments that use effectiveness monitoring and evaluation to generate improved understanding that, in turn, leads to new actions.

Over-interpretation or misinterpretation of the meaning and effect of science findings and knowledge – effective environmental management has its roots in environmental science. As environmental science advances, environmental managers constantly re-interpret their methods in light of the new scientific findings and knowledge. Some participants may choose to over-emphasize the importance of a specific science finding, or they may misinterpret scientific knowledge to advance their values over an opponent's values. EDR leaders can mitigate this by incorporating science panels or management peer-panels into dispute-resolution public events and deliberations. The idea will be to build broad-based public understanding of the content and impact of science findings and knowledge.

Professional arrogance or self-righteous thinking and behavior – professional arrogance assumes that one profession or body of managerial thought is superior to another. Self-righteous thinking is similar because it places one person or group and their values and attitudes superior relative to others. People displaying professional arrogance or holding self-righteous views are capable of dehumanizing and destroying others without responsibility. To be effective, EDR leaders have to create an EDR environment in which all professions and attitudes receive equal value, even if they do not have equal impact in the EDR effort.

Single-resource or single-issue focus – some participants will be concerned about a single resource or environmental condition. They may also choose to focus on one issue, advocating that their issue receive full EDR attention. Although advocates and opponents may see this as a good tactic to express their values, this approach results in a "small pie" effect — there are few choices for the dispute-resolution community. It may also increase "black-and-white" views of the resources and the dispute. EDR practitioners will want to overcome this impediment by building a "bigger pie" and developing community understanding of a broad range of issues and opportunities for consideration.

Scapegoating, blaming, and diminishment – as mentioned in the "unpleasant opponent" impediment, some participants may choose to use scapegoating, blaming, and diminishment as tactics for advancing their values. EDR practitioners should discuss the effects of these tactics early in the dispute-resolution-community building efforts, and they should consciously help the community create norms that oppose these tactics. Then they should objectively confront these tactics when they appear.

Exiting physically, mentally, and emotionally – some participants will choose to exit from EDR efforts by leaving physically or "checking out" emotionally or mentally. Physical exists are sometimes done strategically in order to disrupt the EDR effort, particularly by participants viewed as essential for effective EDR. By doing this, they hope to gain a power-play advantage and force concessions contingent upon their return. Regardless of the exit, EDR leaders should emphasize early and often in the EDR program that exits will damage the potential for success. Later in the EDR effort, leaders should point out that individuals choosing to exit are breaking community norms and agreements.

Building Dispute Prevention Measures into Routine Public and Private Processes

Chapters 12 and 13 of Theory and Principles speak to how we can develop effective EDR strategies, means, and methods to apply to environmental disputes at all spatial and time scales. Under our current system of laws and regulations, federal, state, and local agencies can often only pursue EDR by folding EDR strategies and techniques into existing public environmental-management funding allocation and decision-making efforts. Although they may be frequently involved with government at various levels on environmental affairs, I would encourage businesses and non-governmental organizations to pursue similar EDR-within-decision-making approaches independently.

National Environmental Policy Act decision-making, combined with effective public involvement, such as that promoted by the Institute for Participatory Management and Planning, is common to all federal agencies. Similar reductionist and deterministic planning and decision-making methods are common at state and local levels, too. Public-process managers and decision-makers can build EDR into every step of these approaches, thus maximizing the potential for an implementable decision.

This intrinsic approach is effective for decisions at hand. I have built EDR into my decisions and supported other decision makers repeatedly with good results over 25 years.

Unfortunately, most of these decisions involve discrete changes to the human environment at small scale. Therefore, they do not build long-term, broad-scale, extra-process EDR agreements and actions that could prevent future dispute recycling and other pathological conditions.

Repeated, effective, small-scale EDR efforts do tend to build toward a larger-scale EDR context and can contribute to a self-sustaining EDR culture at many scales, but most participants are often not aware of the effects. In addition, with such an ad hoc EDR approach, personalities play a far greater role in ensuring success than they should. Building EDR institutions and culture can only occur if we do not base them on the efforts of one or a few EDR advocates and practitioners.

I have advocated **citizen-led environmental and decision document preparation** for many years. In this approach, working with government and other experts, citizens voluntarily propose actions, prepare environmental analyses and documents, and develop decision rationales and documentation. Because decisions are citizen-driven, the EDR benefits can be significant if the citizens involved represent a dispute-resolution community.

Visionary/opportunistic decisions offer a different venue for EDR than most National Environmental Policy Act or similar state and local problem-solving-style decisions. People can use all time and spatial scales to make these decisions, and they can formulate the exercises leading up to them. Many visionary/opportunistic decision-making efforts are "zero-based" in nature (starting from "scratch" in the present) and capable of incorporating "forethought" (a technique for describing a desired future in realistic terms). Therefore, planners and decision makers can build EDR into the entire visioning and opportunity effort, and later, they can define them as specific strategies and tasks in any resulting action plan. Private businesses and non-governmental organizations might find this decision-making model more familiar than government-agency employees would find it to be.

Community and Regional Master Planning efforts offer similar opportunities, but some planners and local decision makers might regard building long-term, effective EDR into these efforts with some suspicion. Many would point to present strategies and techniques for public involvement as fulfilling the EDR role, failing to recognize the debilitating effects of issue recycling and other dispute pathologies. Therefore, EDR practitioners and supporters may want to create opportunities for education and advocacy to get effective EDR built into community and regional decision-making efforts.

Although the process is not available nationally, many states offer citizens the right to pursue **initiatives** and **referenda**. An initiative allows citizens to propose a change in state or local laws and regulations, and sometimes in a constitution, by placing a measure on the ballot for public vote. A referendum is a non-binding vote, also taken through a common vote, which provides information for legislators that can then influence their legislative behavior. One disputant in a dispute may try to use an initiative or referendum to exert control. Likewise, however, a dispute-resolution community can use these legislative opportunities to make structural changes agreed to as a part of a resolution.

Environmental Management Systems that comply with the International Standards Organization 14000 requirements could also be a place to incorporate EDR. Like National Environmental Policy Act decision-making, the scope for an Environmental Management System application may be too restrictive for broad-scale EDR; but if the Environmental Management System application contains enough effective EDR elements, it could also contribute to a self-sustaining EDR culture at many scales.

The **World Wide Web** offers great potential for developing EDR understanding and for sharing EDR strategies, methods, and techniques. The Web is the quintessential crossroads for information and the sharing of ideas. Currently, however, EDR-related web sites do not nearly reach the potential that I believe exists for an international EDR consortium.

After the Dispute Resolution Community Disbands

Once the dispute-resolution community and management team, if any, adjourn, EDR practitioners and caring on-lookers may wish **to create an entity to sustain the agreements reached and community stability that has been created**. A review of the techniques list reveals many such techniques that could serve in the way for the long term. These include **ombuds, mediator,** and **referee** programs. Many of these techniques might be explicitly mentioned in agreements so that future disputes can be resolved under them.

Chapter 15: Dispute Communications

This chapter focuses on how practitioners may want to vary communications to fit the dispute stage. Much more extensive discussions of communications can be found in Theory and Principles and throughout earlier chapters of this book.

Consult Community	Diagnose Disputes	Build Prescription	Act	Prevent New Disputes	Monitor and Adjust	Let Go or Re-consult

Previously, I defined dispute composition elements to include means of communication, such as letters or newspapers. I also defined the function and relationship element as including message content. All aspects of EDR depend heavily on communications, keyed to and integrated with EDR outcomes, objectives, and techniques. Because communications and related public-involvement is so critical in dispute-resolution work, this chapter will emphasize communications considerations.

Communications involves the delivery of information, verbal or nonverbal. The delivery can occur in one direction only (experts call this "single-tailed" communication) or be interactive, flowing back and forth among many parties ("two-tailed" communication).

EDR experts frequently use a form of two-tailed communications called "responsive," "effective," "active," or "empathetic" listening. This is a person- and values-affirming process wherein the listener "mirrors" the speaker's statements (repeats them back as precisely as possible), validates the statements made and the values behind them, and empathizes with the speaker by accurately describing their emotions.

Communications can be designed to escalate the impact on and use by targeted audiences. For example, first create basic awareness of EDR; second, build full understanding of its means, methods, and values to society; and third, show how EDR contributes to dispute de-escalation and loss stoppage. EDR practitioners and their communications consultants will exercise choice as regards what to communicate, how often, by what means, and which opponents' and other participants' behaviors are to be affected.

Issues Abatement and Communications

My experience with disputes and dispute escalation is that disputes begin with a narrow values-based disagreement called an "issue." Issues often involve only one subject and as few as two parties. Left unabated, they can escalate into larger, broader, "full-blown" conflicts involving many parties and issues.

Over the years, I have used intensely focused issues-abatement methods to virtually eliminate dispute escalation because single subject, issues-abatement efforts can be more effectively focused on factual misunderstandings than full-blown conflicts with competing and confusing information and interpretations.

Frequently, clarification and clear communication of the facts eliminates or solves issues. Thus managed, the issue never grows into a broad-scale conflict.

I used issues-abatement to essentially eliminate lawsuits from the Alaska Region between 1996 and 2002, for example, and in all but one case involving fire-killed timber salvage on the Umpqua National Forest between 2002 and 2006.

Issues abatement requires excellent, clear, accurate communications and fast response times. In Alaska, I used a daily telephone call that linked regional leaders with field leaders and other professionals for about 20-30 minutes a day. We covered many topics, but we routinely shared information about issues. The source of our initial issue "alert" could be a media or Congressional contact, a phone call from a constituent, a chance meeting with an angry party, or simple intuition about who might be affected by a future event or decision.

From the initial discovery of the issue, we made a series of rapid decisions, which generally involved contacting people to gather more information and then communicating with affected parties orally or in writing.

Our intention was to keep Alaska issues from "going national," and thus, taking the conflict out of our direct ability to manage them and into higher-conflict and higher-cost situations. We correctly believed that keeping the issue local meant keeping our costs minimized, whether financial or delay costs.

Over the course of my years in Alaska, we managed hundreds of issues locally, ranging from simple misunderstandings about a cabin rental to major issues about timber management and sales. One of the most contentious relationships we had to deal with was with the State of Alaska. Across the nation, the tensions and conflicts of differing powers and authorities make natural resource management relationships with states difficult, and the situation is probably most difficult in Alaska, which has been described as a "fiercely independent welfare state" that expects federal handouts and concessions but wherein federal decisions must be submissive to state priorities and values.

When I arrived in Alaska in 1996, a recent incident had highlighted a serious disagreement between the state and the Forest Service over the authority to manage fisheries resources. I had already dealt with the issue in the 1980s, but it had apparently gone unmanaged since.

In the recent case, the state had dispatched a State Trooper to arrest a District Ranger for replacing a culvert on a fish-bearing stream that was on private land but under Forest Service easement. The Forest Service fielded a law enforcement officer who would have prevented the arrest of the ranger and instead arrested the State Trooper for interfering in the actions of a federal official. The dispute had been simmering for decades and came down to whether the Forest Service had to have a state permit for doing such work as a culvert replacement on a fish-bearing stream, a classic contest between state and federal powers. Our attorneys said the state had no such powers on federal land, but State Title 16 said they did.

I knew of other state-federal issues that had been simmering for as long as this one, including coastal zone management, land occupancy fees, riparian- and tidal-zone access management, and subsistence uses by rural residents. I asked my staff to begin working on agreements with the state that would resolve the issues of Title 16, Coastal Zone Management, fees for occupancy, and riparian and tidal zone access management. Between 1996 and 2002, we resolved the first three with signed memoranda of understanding and agreements meant to mitigate or eliminate the disputes.

The tidal zone access-management agreement was not achieved in part because it had not then escalated into a prominent issue, or as some attorneys refer to issues, it had not "ripened." Subsistence management could only be partially handled by the Forest service because the authority for managing issues state-wide rested with another agency, the U.S. Fish and Wildlife Service. The Forest Service was able to manage and mitigate subsistence issues within southeast and south-central Alaska only insofar as our limited authorities would permit, mainly handling local user disputes informally.

Full-Blown Conflict Resolution and Communications

As issues escalate into broader, multi-issue, full-blown conflicts and the numbers of participants increase, the intensity and complexity of communications also grows. To be effective, EDR practitioners have to develop an effective communications program that deals with conventional communications channels, such as the print and electronic media, and unconventional channels, such as informal information networks within communities and organizations.

In cases of full-blown conflict, I first begin by describing and graphically displaying the issues structure. Generally, the structure is composed of several (perhaps dozens) of issues, many of which "connect" in some way to other issues. The connections can be based on subject, including ecological, economic, and social topics and relationships. They can also be based on analysis or data interpretation; for example, the data about conditions at one ecological scale might offer insight into conditions at other scales or at other places with similar conditions.

Another connection is based on the communities of interest, place, tradition, and fate. People define issues and, in some ways, issues define people, so a thorough understanding of people's values and how they are part of values-based communities is useful in order to describe the many issues embedded in the full-blown conflict.

Once I have displayed the issues and assigned communities and individuals by issue, I confirm the connections and relationships with the opponents and other participants, adding information at each interaction until I have a thorough understanding of issues and values. I then use a team to set an order for addressing each issue and to begin work on issue abatement. Some issues are dealt with concurrently; some wait until other issues are managed so that data needs and values preferences can be addressed in the most effective order.

I deconstruct the full-blown conflicts into component issues, recognizing, acknowledging, and confirming the connections among the issues and among the participants. I then address each issue in an ordered manner, reflective of the relationships among the issues and participants. Ultimately, all issues get addressed and the full-blown conflict is resolved.

As issue abatement moves forward, communications must be adapted as each issue is addressed, for the participants and their desires and abilities as well as for the overall EDR effort, including the priority for sustained team efforts.

Crisis Control and Communication

Many participants in a conflict (and people concerned about the conflict but not directly engaged or affected) are able to predict the onset of a crisis. Even if a pattern drives the crisis, such as a fuel build up in a forest leading to extensive, intense wildfire, the forest will be changed for all time as it goes through a fire-driven evolution. The more the fire is out of the range of natural variation, the more profound the crisis and its aftermath.

Communications just before, during, and just after a crisis are profoundly different than those during a full-blown conflict. At this point, the "least preferred alternative" has occurred and will dominate events until it runs its course.

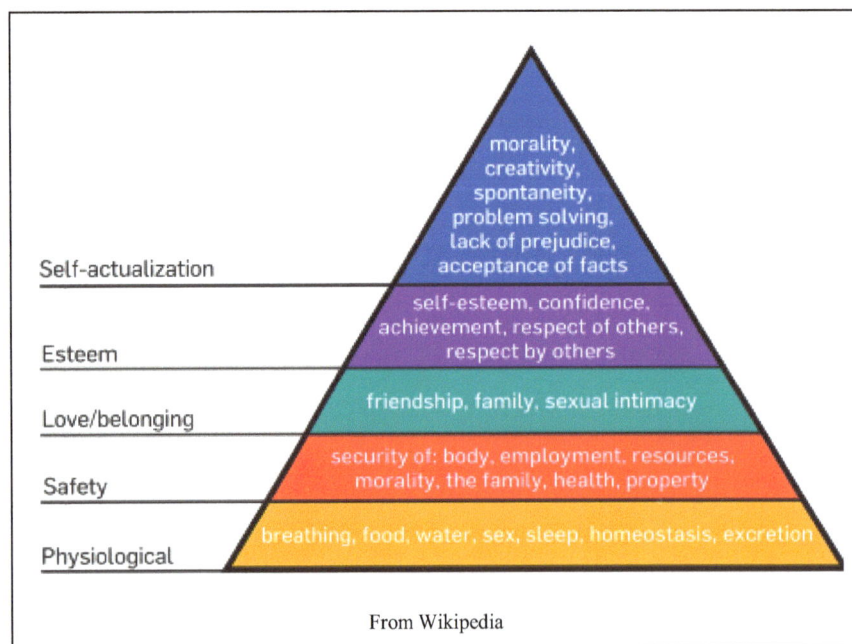

From Wikipedia

During the crisis "pulse," communications tend to follow Maslow's hierarchy of needs from bottom to top. Crisis communications focus first on individual and community survival and cohesion, and then expand to the loss-grieving, re-assembly and reunification of communities, and the early-recovery portion of the aftermath.

Once blaming begins to dominate communications, EDR practitioners should know that they have entered into the crisis' aftermath and are in transition to a new set of conditions, actors, and issues.

For example, in cases where wildland firefighters are killed in the line of duty, blame can escalate rapidly and intensely.

Recovery Management and Communications

Once the crisis is over, actions and communications tend to focus on recovery, restoration, and achieving a new "normal" state. Sometimes the new norm is very similar to the past, as it would be if a house is rebuilt to look just as it did before a hurricane blew it down. Sometimes, the new norm is significantly different and yet similar to the past, such as in the case of divorce or spousal death. Other times, the new norm is a complete alteration, such as the explosion of Krakatoa or Mt. St. Helens.

While much attention will be paid to assigning blame for the crisis, the communications that people are most interested in are those related to transition and recovery. These include information about the location and nature of desired services, resources, family, and friends, means to communicate with authorities in charge of recovery resources and services, and the timing of actions and events.

Communication Art and Science

Because EDR program success often rests significantly on the means and content of communications, EDR leaders and practitioners have good reason to gain expertise in communications. They may possess these skills themselves for look for expertise within the dispute-resolution community. From speakers to proof-readers, some of the most effective communication experts I've ever used were volunteers from the community who simply wanted to help the dispute-resolution effort.

Practitioners may want to become familiar with "neurolinguistics," which is the study of the neural functions in the brain that control the comprehension, production, and language acquisition[30]. Use of neurolinguistics may increase communications effectiveness significantly in both the selection of means (compositional factor) and design of the message (functional or relationship factor).

---

[30] http://www.holisticonline.com/hol_neurolinguistic

Chapter 16: Adjusting and Ending the Program

Monitoring dispute resolution progress, making adjustments, and ending the program are closely related. The close relationship exists because when sufficient goals are met, the program is at an end or re-consultation with the community becomes timely.

| Consult Community | Diagnose Disputes | Build Prescription | Act | Prevent New Disputes | Monitor and Adjust | Let Go or Re-consult |

When goals and objectives are explicitly stated in the program prescription, dispute-resolution community members and EDR practitioners should be able to monitor progress. They can check off each objective as it is accomplished. If selected techniques fail to perform and achieve the objectives they support, they can be modified or replaced. If objectives seem off-target after a while, they, too, can be modified or replaced.

If goals and objectives are not explicitly stated in the prescription, as might occur with a single-issue, distress-pathway dispute, then EDR practitioners will want to consult disputants on an on-going basis. This is a critical communication focused specifically on whether disputants have reached acceptable levels of satisfaction. When they have, and prevention of further disputes has been clearly discussed, the resolution is ended or refocused on another dispute.

The process for deciding whether objectives and techniques are performing adequately should be built into the prescription and reviewed regularly. This work is a dispute-resolution community function, led by community leaders or the EDR practitioners. Similar to group norms and guidelines, goals, objectives, and supporting techniques should be displayed for a participants to see. Posters, power-points, table mats, and report sections might all be used for this purpose.

EDR leaders and practitioners may also wish to review and adaptively use the USIECR Evaluation Framework[31] to evaluate the success of their program. This framework is particularly applicable at larger ecological scales but it may be used at any scale. The Framework has four major elements: Desired Process Conditions, Expected Process Dynamics, End-of-Process Outcomes, and Impacts.

Before beginning use of the Framework, practitioners should remember that USIECR uses a more limited model than set forth in Theory and Principles and this book. USIECR's processes also focus on a more limited techniques set, generally confining their program to mediation and formal agreements.

To address issues about closing out the dispute-resolution community, readers might want to review pages 162 -164.

---

[31] Conflict Resolution Quarterly. *Environmental Conflict Resolution Practice and Performance: An Evaluation Framework.* Orr, Patricia J., Emerson, Kirk, and Keyes, Dale L. Vol. 25, No. 3, Spring 2008. pp. 283-301.

Appendix A: Some Useful EDR Definitions

Crisis — an event (or series of related events) that results in a permanent, significant change in the structure, composition, or functions and relationships associated with a conflict; picture reaching a ridge between two watersheds: by crossing over, you enter a new watershed — a crisis is a "watershed" event. Loss of control by conflict participants is a characteristic of a crisis[32].

Dispute Escalation— increasing levels of strife usually exhibiting expanding numbers of issues and participants[33].

Dispute Progression—dispute escalation from issues to full-blown conflict to crisis to recovery in the aftermath of crisis.

Issue — a topic about which there is more than one opinion or position; usually a narrow, values-based dispute among two (or a few) parties leading, if unmanaged, to full-blown conflict. Dispute abatement at this stage is the most cost-efficient option, although abatement usually does not usually attempt to mitigate or eliminate the basic values conflict among parties[34].

Environmental Dispute — person-to-person, group-to-group, or nature-to-person/group strife marked by a power struggle between parties with well-defined opposing positions and different desired outcomes[35].

EDR leader – a member of the dispute community or community at large who helps convene the EDR community, defines work goals, priorities, and content, and then creates focus and urgency for the people doing EDR work.

EDR participant – someone who has decided to join the EDR community, commit to its ethics and norms, and work actively to end gridlock.

EDR practitioner – a lay-person or professional who conducts environmental dispute resolution activities. Practitioners focus primarily on assisting the EDR community with its development, using a diagnostic-prescriptive method to develop an EDR program plan, and then helping the community implement that program**Environmental justice** -- the equitable distribution of ecological services such as clean air and water, nutritious and safe food, and recreation while avoiding the inequitable imposition of environmental impacts such as pollutants, desertification, and disease.

Environmental peace – the condition of harmony between people and nature and among the people who live with nature.

---

[32] IBID. Greek — "to decide"

[33] IBID. French — "to increase in extent, volume, number, amount, intensity of scope"

[34] IBID. French — "to come, go, or rise out of"

[35] *Webster's New Collegiate Dictionary,* G&C Merriam Co., Springfield, MA. 1979. Latin — "to discuss"

Full-blown Conflict — a dispute with many issues and participants as well as complex interactions and communications; some conflicts exhibit accumulation of issues and participants that lead to crisis[36].

Recovery — the new structure, composition, and functions or relationships that exist after a crisis; if recovery is handled effectively, long-standing and recycling disputes may be reduced or eliminated[37].

There are many ways to define disputes. Many of these derive from studies of war and international diplomacy practices and cannot be easily applied to civil disputes in America. Other definitions are driven by practitioners who advocate a particular method and try to apply it in every management context.

In the two books, I deliver a model focused on environmental disputes in America. More importantly, the model allows EDR practitioners to select the right techniques for their specific situation. No "cookie-cutter" approaches allowed. I focus on four broad "mental models," or "pathways," that I have found useful in my work over many years. These are:

    Distress – the internal struggles that individuals and small groups go through to resolve personal-values disputes.[38] EDR can help create positive outcomes, turning "distress" into "eustress.[39]"

    Scandal* – parties call for societal rejection of the values or behaviors of an individual or a group in order to create conformance with societal values or norms.[40]

    Anarchy* – individuals or groups reject a societal value or majority cultural view with the intention to re-order some commonly held values or behaviors or society as a whole.[41]

    Catastrophe – the undesirable and unacceptable effects of a natural event, or the breakdown of the built environment, on humans and society.[42]

      *I am broadening the meaning of the words "scandal" and "anarchy" in this book. My intention is to emphasize the commonalities of the concepts embodied in the pathways and reframe the readers' understanding of dispute progression.

The four pathways tend to mirror how most environmental disputes are structured, articulated, and fought out in our society. I find that the pathways approach allows participants to focus on acceptable outcomes and recovery more quickly and effectively.

---

[36] IBID. Latin — "to strike together"
[37] IBID. Latin — "to receive or retain"
[38] *Webster's New Collegiate Dictionary,* G&C Merriam Co., Springfield, MA. 1979. Latin — "to bind or seize"
[39] www.eustress.com
[40] IBID. Latin — "stumbling block or offense"
[41] IBID. Greek — "having no ruler"
[42] IBID. Greek — "to overturn"

It is true that disputes along the four pathways may contain interdependent elements or even overlap. However, a particular dispute is usually characterized by one of the four pathways, making the distinction valuable to people seeking resolution.

In short, using the pathways approach, a dispute can be effectively defined. The definition then makes resolution more efficient and focused.

Appendix B: EDR Program Plan Template

Building the program plan requires that practitioners bring together people and opportunity. Program plans often have to be redone several times over the course of EDR implementation. Here is a template for building the program plan:

Step 1 -- Complete Dispute Diagnosis (from Chapter 6; use Chapter 1-5 as background)

Subject

1. What is (are) the topic(s) of this dispute?

Parameters

2. Who are the participants and what are their values concerning this dispute?	Opponents Caring onlookers Dispute community Dispute-resolution community
3. What stage is the dispute in and why?	Issue Full-blown conflict Crisis Recovery
4. What pathway(s) is the dispute traveling and why?	Distress Scandal Anarchy Catastrophe
5. What are the contributing factors?	Structural Compositional Functional Relationship
6. What are the context and history of the dispute?	Context History

		Connections to other disputes
		Past communications
		Dispute scale (attach maps if needed)
7. What are the threats inherent in this dispute?	Risks	
	Vulnerabilities	
	Consequences	
	No-action and no-resolution consequences	
8. What are the impediments to success held by the opponents and essential participants?	Impediments by participant	
9. Who are the powerful people who must support or consent to the EDR effort for it to be successful?	At dispute's scale	
	At lower scale(s)	
	At higher scale(s)	

Step 2 -- Set Priorities (from Chapter 7; use Chapters 1-6 as background)

This section describes which of the 16 cells in diagnostic matrix (stage and pathway) should be addressed in the EDR effort. The choices should be supported by the context and history, and reflect understandings of the structural, compositional, or functional and relationship causes. Practitioners should also describe threats associated with each listed item and impediments associated with each opponent who cares about the item.

The list should be prioritized by the dispute-resolution community; optimally, the list should be force-ranked. Practitioners may find that much consensus is not possible because of differing value-preference scales or dispute intensity. However, broader grouping such as "high," "medium," and "low" may be possible and can provide a beginning. In high-intensity full-blown conflict or crisis situations, leaders may have to set the priorities quickly and further refine them with the dispute-resolution community later.

Step 3 -- State the EDR Strategy (from Chapter 7)

Describe the strategy, including the EDR vision, as explicitly stated by the dispute-resolution community if the members have been recruited.

Step 4 -- Establish EDR Direction (from Chapter 7; use Chapters 9-12 as background)

Goal 1:

    Objectives to support goal 1:

    1.1)

    1.2)

Goal 2:

    Objectives to support Goal 2:

    2.1)

    2.2)

        *Evaluation Criteria
        ** Success Measure

And so forth until all goals and objectives (including evaluation criteria and success measures) are set.

Step 5 -- Select EDR Techniques (from Chapter 8; use Chapters 9-12 as background)

To support:

Objective 1.1)

    Technique —

    Technique —

Objective 1.2)

    Technique —

    Technique —

Objective 2.1)

Technique —

Technique —

Objective 2.2)

Technique —

Technique —

Step 6 -- Set the Implementation Schedule

	Month	Month	Month	Month	Month

Technique

    Task
    Task
    Task
    Task

Technique

    Task
    Task
    Task
    Task

Technique

    Task
    Task
    Task
    Task

Technique

    Task
    Task
    Task
    Task

Step 7 -- Engage the Dispute-Resolution Community (connect the lists of people and organizations to the tasks and timing of the implementation schedule)

	Name	Contact	Issue(s)	Constituents
Place				
Interest				
Tradition				
Fate				

Step 8 – Contact and Engage People Holding Power Essential to EDR Success

Name	Position	Issue(s)	Agreements	Contact Schedule

Appendix C – Principal Publications by James Caplan

Unless otherwise noted, Caplan was sole author of the following publications:

- Umpqua National Forest Mission, Vision, Principles, and Management Guidelines 2001-2002 [co-author with forest management team, lead]

- Alaska Region Strategic Priorities, Alaska Natives Emphasis Item, December 2000 [co-author, lead]

- Alaska Region Strategies for "Collaborative Stewardship," "Budget," and "Integrated Information," August 1996-97, [co-author, lead]

- "New Perspectives for Sustainable Natural Resources Management", Ecological Applications, August 1992 [co-author]

- "Striding into Elephant Country: Exploring New Ground for Planning and Management in Protected Areas," The George Wright FORUM, Spring 1992

- "Sustaining Communities Through Sustained Ecosystems: Experience from the Bridger-Teton National Forest Land and Resource Management Plan in Northwestern Wyoming" to the Western Planners Conference, 1992

- "New Perspectives in Forest Management: Are We Going Over the Waterfall in the Same Canoe?" Proceedings of the Southern Forest Economics Workshop, Washington, D.C., February 1991

- "Fostering Credibility to Build Public Support", Journal of Soil and Water Conservation, Winter 1991

- "Some Thoughts on Bacteria, Planners, and Rumors of Mother Nature's Death" Environmental Planning Quarterly, Winter 1991

- Record of Decision, Bridger-Teton National Forest Land and Resource Management Plan Final Environmental Impact Statement, February, 1990

- Bridger-Teton National Forest Land and Resource Management Plan and Final Environmental Impact Statement, November 1989 [co-author and editor]

- "Point-Counterpoint," a response to a Readers Digest article about Alaska Region management, published and distributed to key groups and Congress, 1986

- Alaska Region Law Enforcement Plan, Approved 1984 [co-author, editor]

- Various Analyses of the Impacts of Pending Legislation on National Forest Management in Alaska, 1981-1984

- Assessments of Annual Legislative Programs for Congress, 1981-1984

- Public Comment Analyses and Narratives for Several Plans, Planning Reports, and Environmental Documents, including the Tongass Land Management Plan Evaluation Report {1984), the Alaska Region comments on the 1985 Draft RPA Program {1984), the Alaska Regional Guide {1983), the "Amendments 2,3 and 4"

Environmental Impact Statement for the U.S. Borax Development at Quartz Hill {1983), and the Draft Regional Plan {1982) [co-author and editor]

- "Some Tips on Effective Coordination," Forest Service Internal Report, 1983

- "Seven Common Planning Errors and What to do About Them," Forest Planning, August, 1982

- The Eastern Region Draft Plan and Environmental Statement, "Issues" and "Public Comment" Sections, 1980-1981

- Conflict Management and Crisis Control: A Manager's Guide, unpublished manuscript. 1980

- "A Play Script of the Land Management Planning and Public Participation Process", 1980

- "Planners and Involvers," a weekly, informal newsletter for planners and information Specialists on the National Forests, 1980

- "Putting the Pieces Together," a Brochure on the Regional Planning Process, 1980

- The "Eastern Region Planner" Newsletter Series, 1979-80

- The Public Comment Portion of Alaska Region's Final Environment Impact Statement: Withdrawal Request Under FLPMA Section 204 C for National Lands in Alaska, 1980 co-author]

- Wyoming Geothermal Institutional Handbook: A User's Guide of Agencies, Regulations, Permits, and Aids for Geothermal Development, 1980

- Big Horn Basin. Wyoming: Area Development Plan (Geothermal), 1980

- A Registry of Institutions Offering Services to Handicapped Wyomingites, Published by the State of Wyoming, Division of Vocational Rehabilitation, 1979

- Master's Thesis: Implementing Sexual Reorientation Services for Disabled Wyomingites, An Institutional Plan Submitted to the State of Wyoming, 1979

- Report: "Some Suggestions for Effective Planning Coordination in Wyoming", Submitted to the State Planning Coordinator's Office, 1978

- Report: "Trends in Wyoming Voter Registration", Submitted to Representative Copenhaver, Wyoming State Legislature, 1977

www.ingramcontent.com/pod-product-compliance
Lightning Source LLC
Chambersburg PA
CBHW060813270326
41929CB00003B/29